ALPHA BET A TEST
LANGUAGE IN THE ACT OF DISAPPEARING
THE EYE AM EYE ASEMIC ANTHOLOGY

INTRODUCTION BY DAVID NADEAU

PUBLISHER'S FOREWORD BY PAUL A. TOTH

Published in the United States of America
First Electronic Release: April 2015
ISBN:
Eye Am Eye Books: http://www.EyeAmEye.org

INTRODUCTION BY DAVID NADEAU: *DOWN TO THE ARCHIVES*

1 • PEDIMENT OF THE NUMBER

The gesture of the hand, clairvoyant, ecstatic, expresses the metaphysical intuition of the absolute: a strangely ornate cross, knightly emblem. In the electromagnetic grimoires, the unexpected hieroglyphs and the complicated diagrams reflect the alteration of the fog, generate other prodigious or disturbing atmospheric phenomena

(the favorable signs engraved on the sky by the sword of a red planet,
the last pre-Columbian cyclone,
the mercurial waves,
the membranous storms built by the plumage of the rocks,
the axis of the fog,
the ridicule wind, which is a pestilential remedy).

Represented by those few silent but effective signs of affiliation, the secret complicity, created between some who wish to remake the human understanding, forms the germ of a future civilization. The natural number torn in every direction, from the side of the the spirit's anniversary, extends itself to the faculties of the seraphim. Metatron Tetragrammaton.

2 • ELECTROMAGNETIC GILGAMESH

When traveling in magical imagination, he remembers the primordial myths, distant extensions of past existences. The hallucinatory textures of some rock surfaces tell him the mythological battles that took place in the early time and the consequences of which are still felt today, unbeknownst to us, in our disenchanted world. The gaze becomes tactile.

3 • ASEMY OR POLYSEMY?

Visit to the subterranean laboratory before its collapse; here, you can still see the occult archives of the subconscious, the complicated charts whose meaning is to be reinvented. This algebra of wonders summarizes the laws of harmony between the different parts of the universe. The multiple diagrams illustrate especially the cosmic cycles of destruction and creation, the new and surrealist worlds revealed by current particle physics, the crossing of the numbers that are tied to each other, the cosmogonies in ruins. Fallen out of the lips of Thoth, the asemic characters create the world, destroy and recreate it. Henri Michaux was born of this globe of experimental alphabet. The syllables fall into the moving abyss. The hypnagogic hallucinations try to decipher the bark of the proteins. The only microscopic poem is floating in a cytoplasm of pleasing appearance. The vacuum appears textured up to hyper-acuity. Christian Dotremont bears the armorial bearings of the morning, in the intimate penumbra of the language. The secret diplomacy of these initiated creators and their companions prepares the advent of a civilization both anarchist and animist.

4 • DREAM OF FEBRUARY THE 13TH 2006, AT 8 HOURS IN THE MORNING

I'm sitting on my bed with an empty bowl of soup in front of me. Small stones of bright colors come out of my mouth, falling in small clusters from behind my uvula. I filled the bowl with the stones of various shapes. I have my hands full and I look admiringly their beautiful bright colors and various patterns. There is a triangular blue stone on which is drawn a yellow pattern resembling an Arabic letter. I drew it upon waking, after noting the dream, with the intention of achieving an object that would look as much as possible like this fascinating asemic rock.

DAVID NADEAU has always been interested in symbols, corner table doodles, enigmatic graffiti. His asemic practice has developed under the influence of the "images interpreted" by the surrealist activist and experimenter Craig S Wilson. This technique involves to move the illustrated sheet placed on the copier glass while it is running, in order to get undulations, stretchings and symmetries of the original image. More recently, the practice of the graphics editor GIMP provides to David a fascinating way to alter images and texts. Thus, *An Emblem of Peril* is the result of the modification of a photograph showing books in a library with a distortion tool from GIMP, named "Polar coordinates." Contact: mercuriussulphur@gmail.com.

PUBLISHER'S FOREWORD BY PAUL A. TOTH

The term "asemic" defies definition, for any definition would confine the asemic to a *possible* act. The asemic act *is* impossible, failure a precondition of its success, for it portrays the evasion of portrayal.

The asemic would capture language in the act of disappearing were its goal not impossible, yet succeeds by its inevitable failure. It lets us know that even the communication of our desperation is gone before we express it.

The asemic depicts dislocation. The asemic map is not the territory; it's not even a map. Of what use is it? None whatsoever. Nothing could be less utilitarian than the asemic map, which could only plot a vacation from a restless existence in one's home town to another town in which one would feel equally restless in a place that looks just like home. The traveler can't wait to flee home from the place that looked and felt just like home.

Wherever you go, you were already there, gone before you arrived; the moment you depart, you've already returned.

Everyone *lives* this strange asemic world. We clutch, and climb, or so it seems, yet we suspect we're being moved along as if on escalators, forever escalating above and beyond all we think we know. We may gradually resort to nostalgia, recalling some moment we think we at least *believed* we knew something...anything. When we recall that moment as accurately as possible, we remember that we didn't believe it then, either: We *thought* we'd believe it in the future...right now...but we're all the more uncertain.

We recede from ourselves the more we peer at the mirror. In fact, we peer at a reflection of a stranger but also a *peer*...somebody reflective of us but never exactly so.

The psychoanalyst Jacques Lacan proposed – rightfully so, I believe – that our first glimpse of ourselves in a mirror becomes the last moment of our having any *sense* of wholeness.

Until then, a child blindly constructs from various cues what will become the *idea* of identity, yet that idea was already under construction in *preconception*, for if a couple *decides* to conceive a child, they begin formulating who and what that child will be before conception occurs. They draw the first blueprint.

Once born, the child becomes a kind of idiot architect, unable to read the parental blueprint or realize it was drawn by others. The child blindly draws another blueprint atop the first. Identity rises like a misconstrued and misconstrued building. One day, the child sees a reflection and says, "I'm myself!" That's the first and last time anyone hasn't the urge to say, "I don't feel quite like myself. What happened to *me*?"

Identity, names and labels are the essential elements of the asemic and represented not on a "periodic table but a "table of the ellipsis."

In the pieces that follow, any apparent message may appear coded, smeared, hieroglyphic, calligraphic, hidden, or in the form of an unknown, forgotten or aborted language. Every message immediately falls prey to entropy and disintegration. The message is that the message isn't even a message.

Identity, names and labels disassemble themselves like technological objects retreating from their intended use not only *back* to the exploded view of their preexistence as illustrated in assembly manuals but beyond even that...beyond the engineering of their birth and their junkyard aftermath.

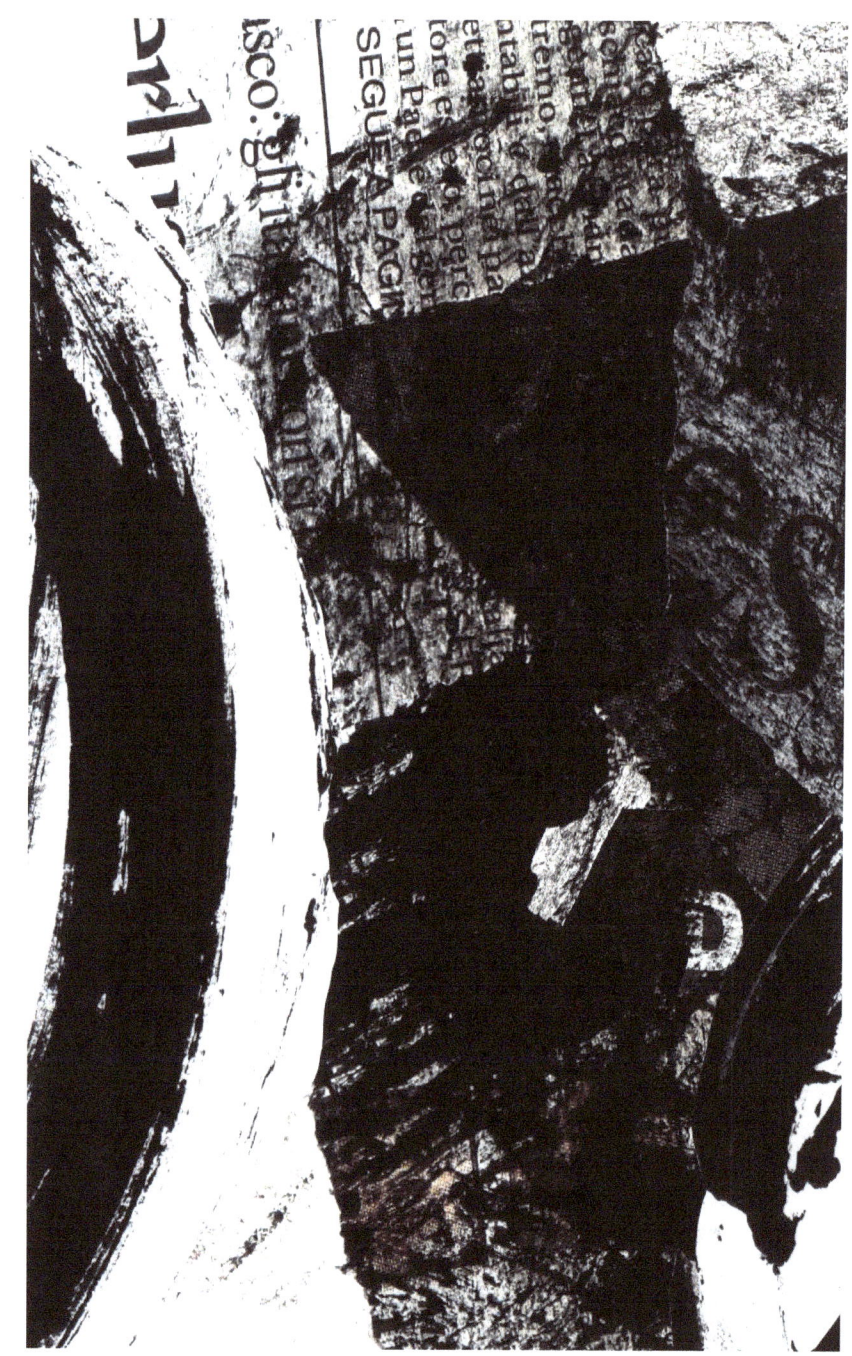

Francesco Aprile: Ende Neu

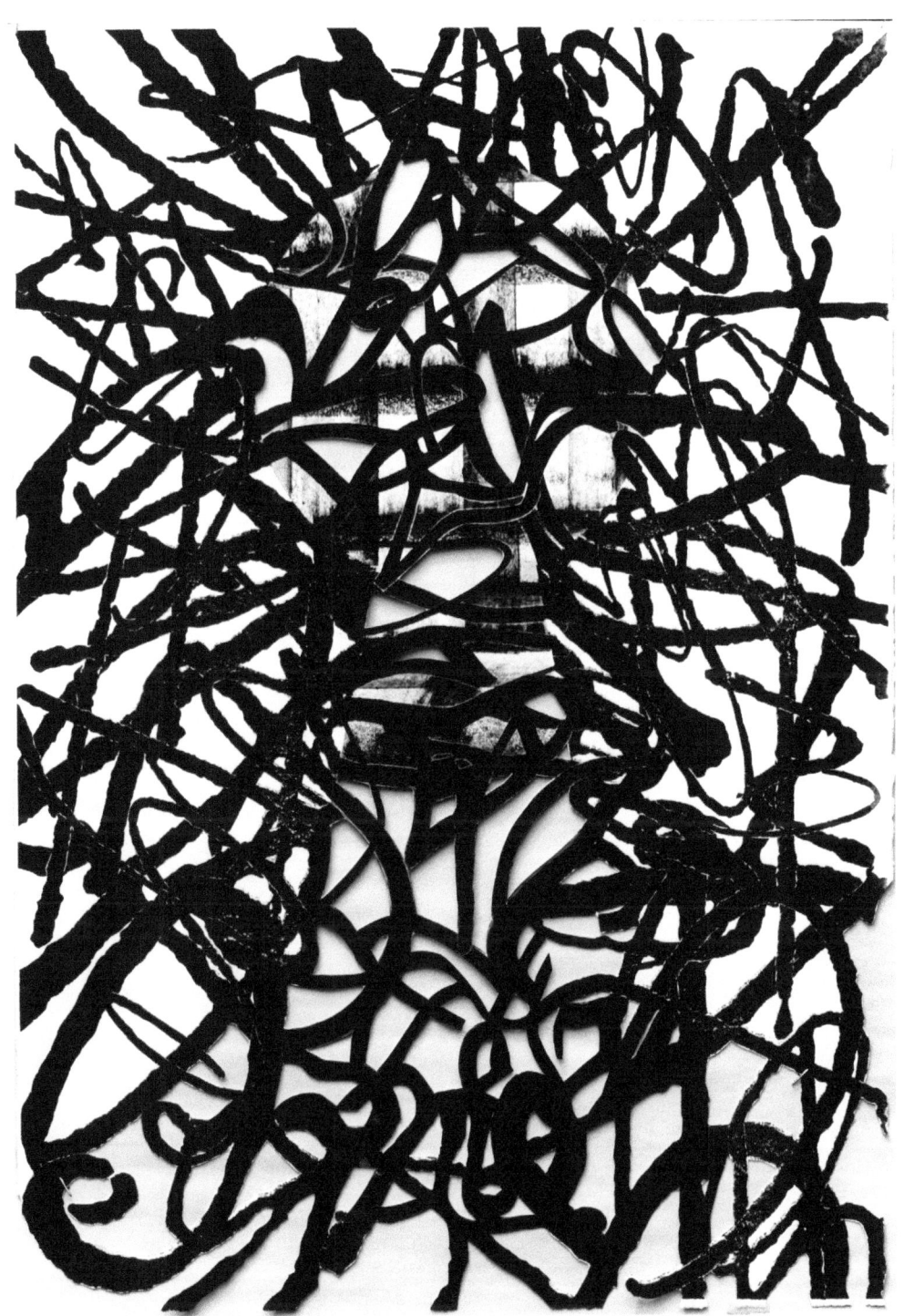

Ian S. Cross: Mother Tongue

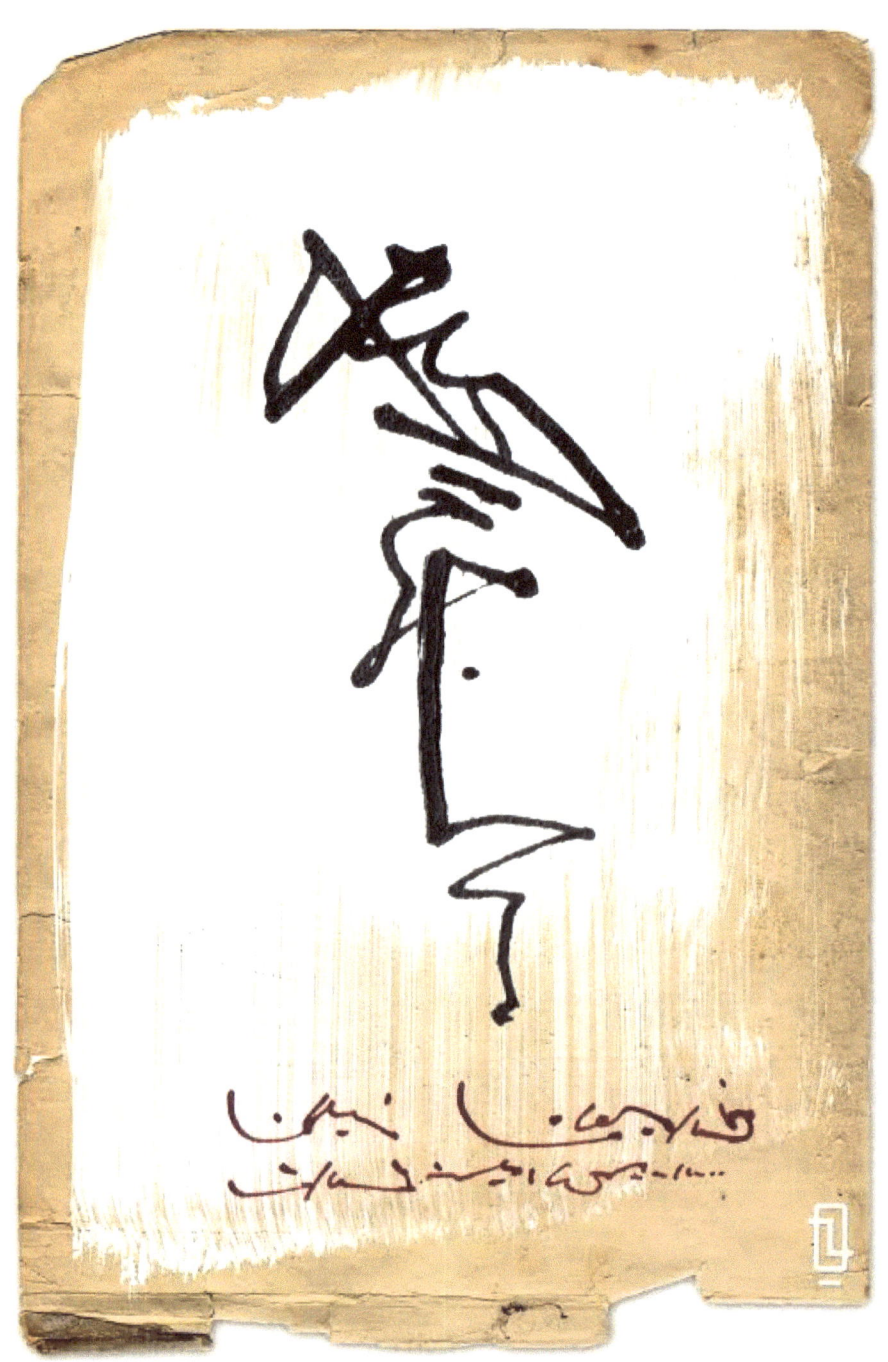

Christopher Skinner: Untitled

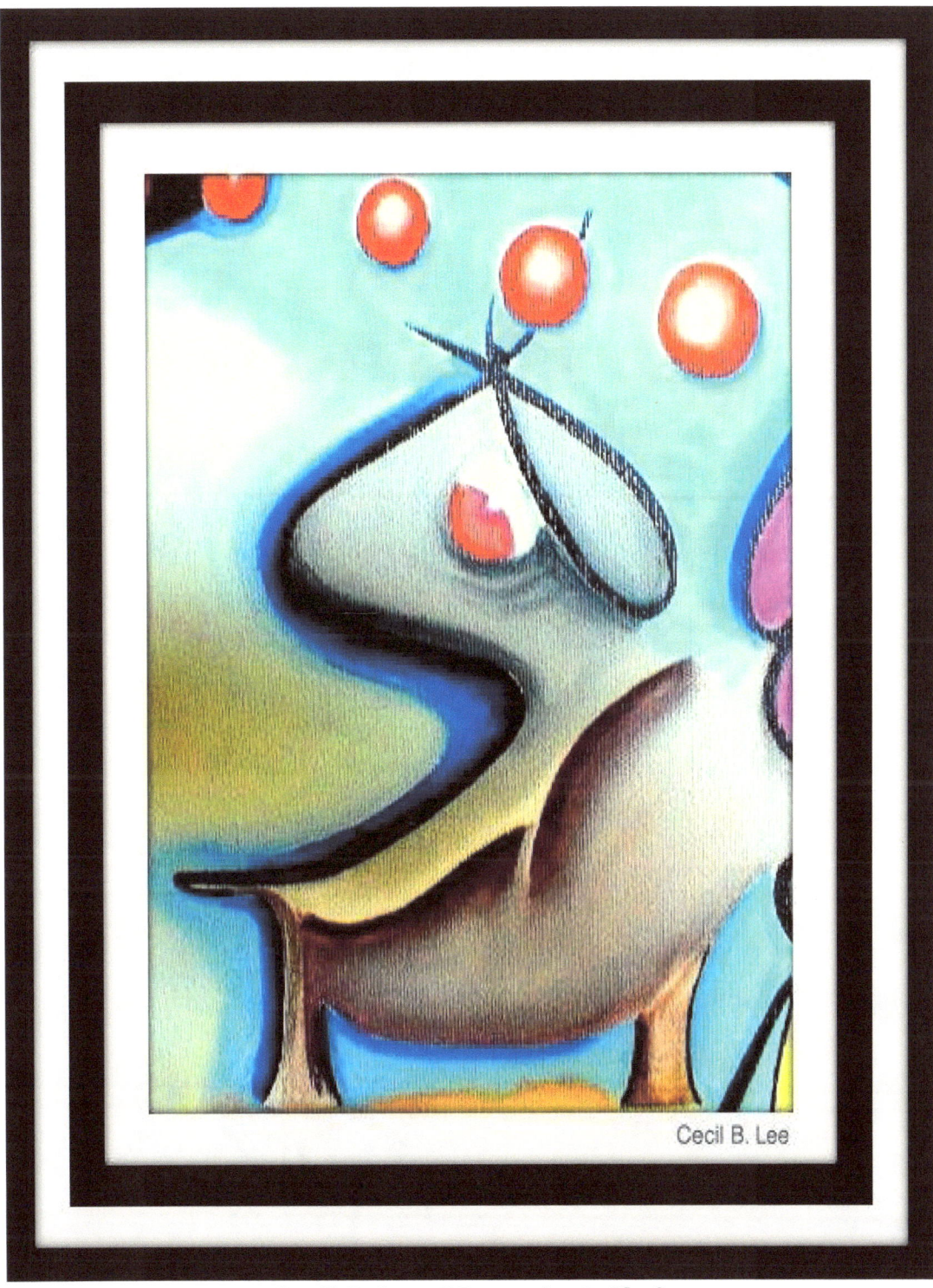

Cecil B. Lee: Mouse In A Chair

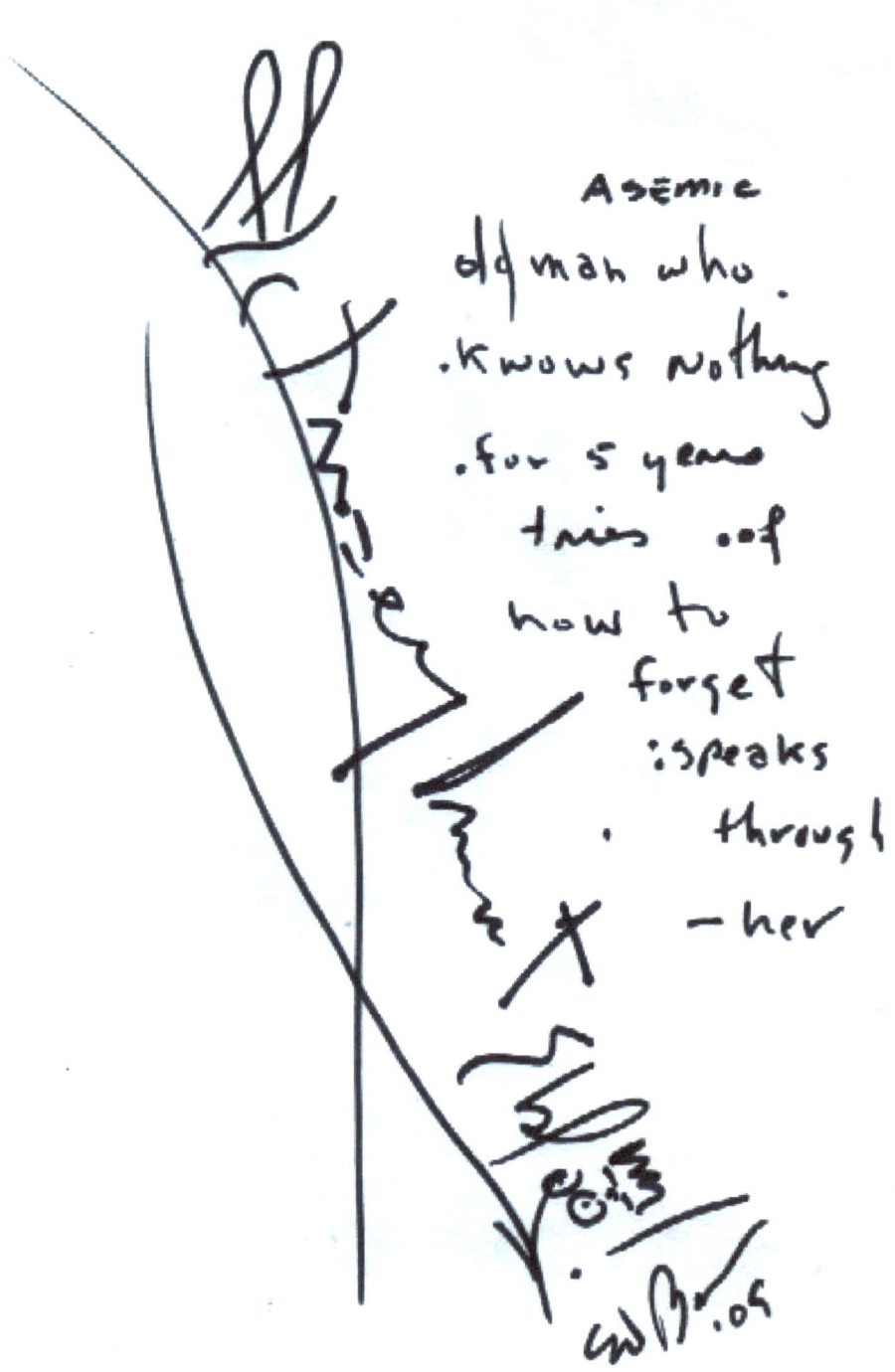

Ed Baker: Old Man

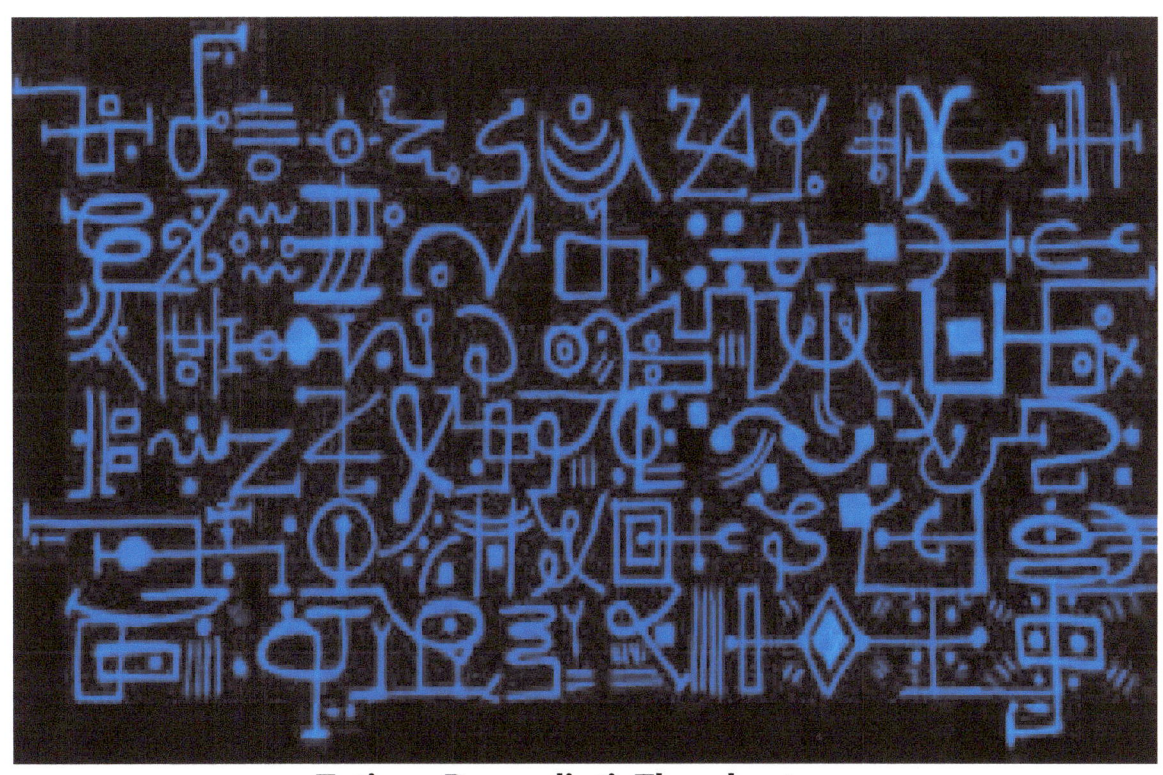

Tatiana Roumelioti: Thunderstorm

Amanda Earl: Cursive 2

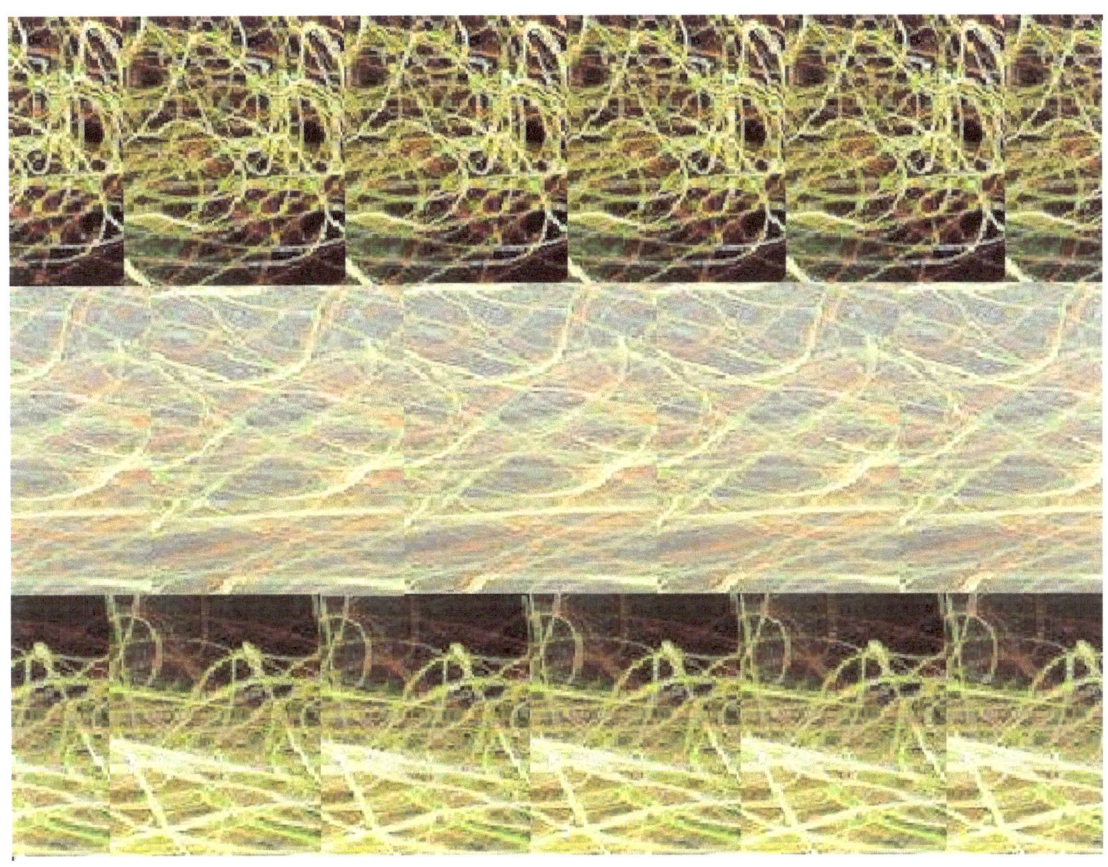

Ali Znaidi: Shades Of Joy

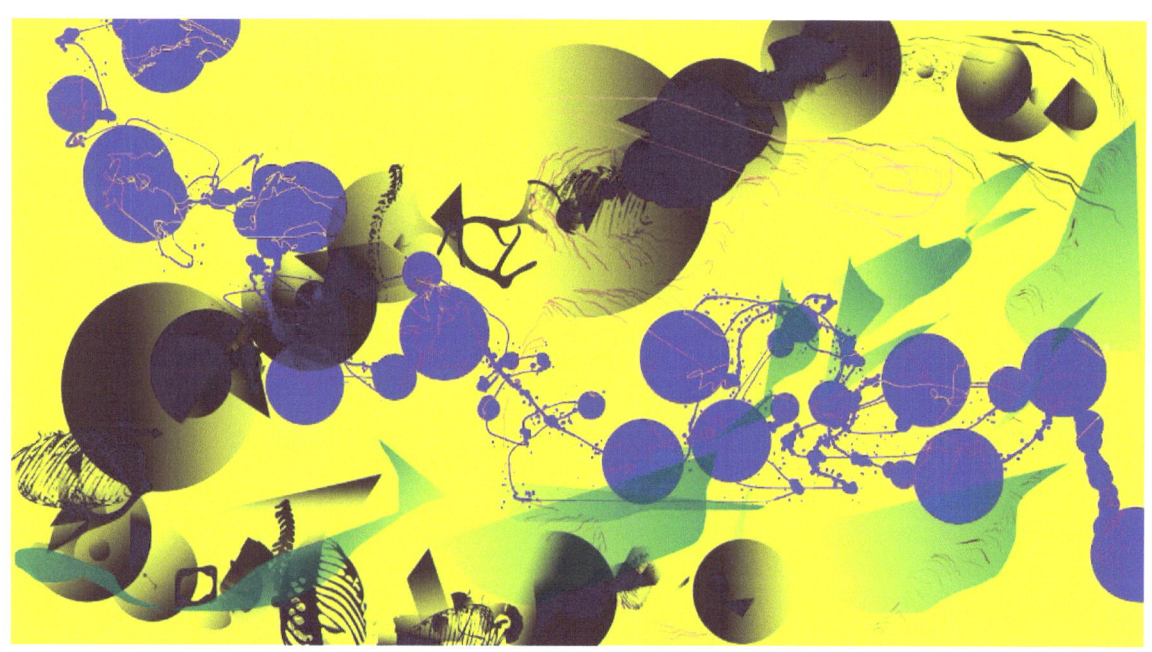

Gheorghe Marian Neguțu: Talking About Myself

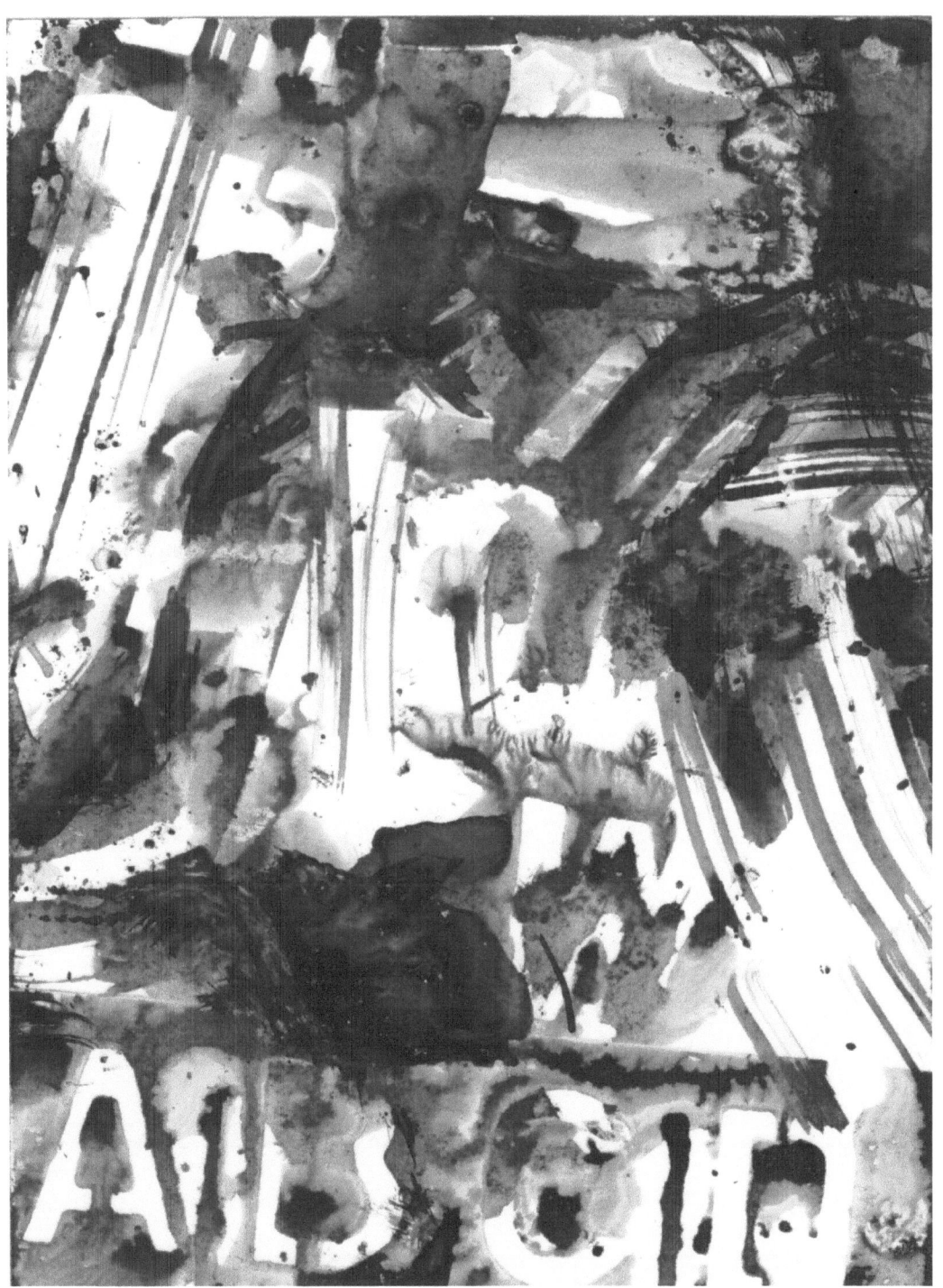

Gregg Simpson: Micromorphology-30

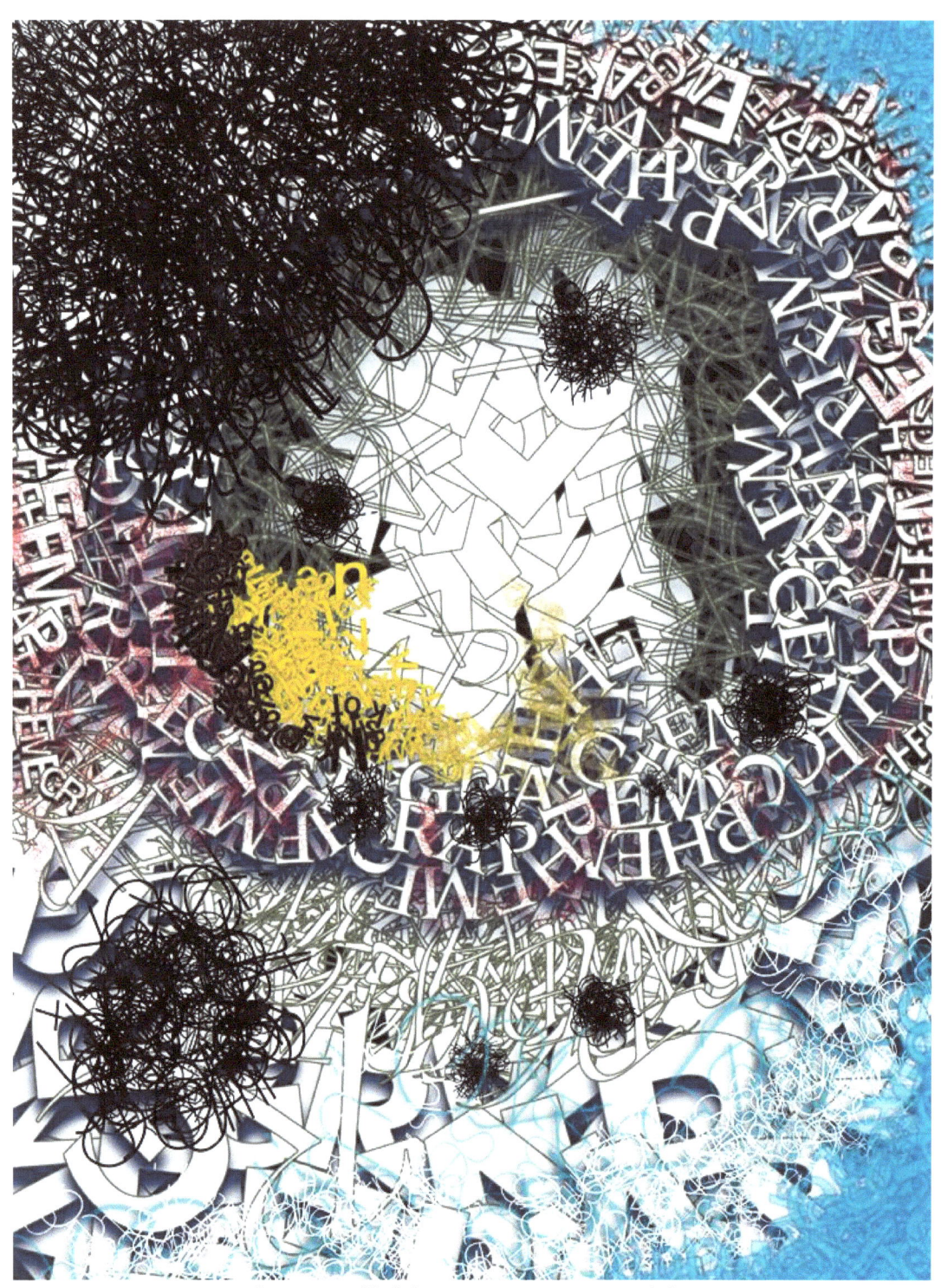

Nico Vassilakis: Letter Composition

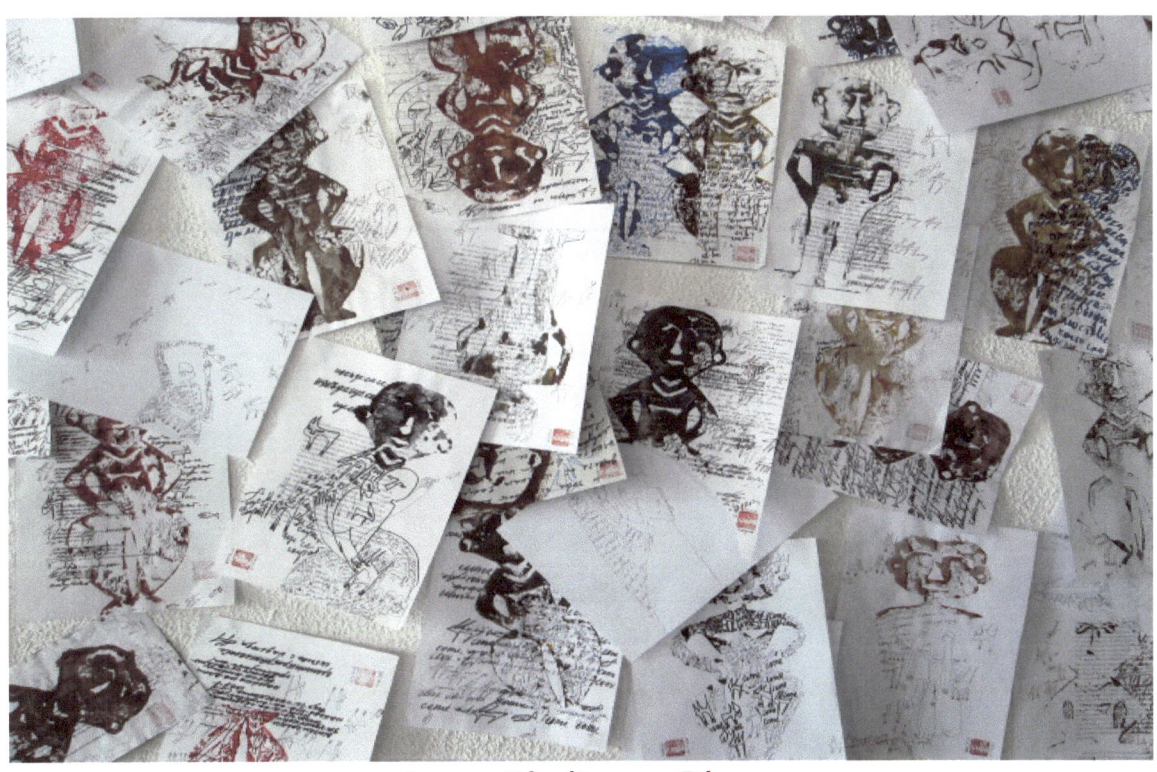

Laura Dimitrova: Diary

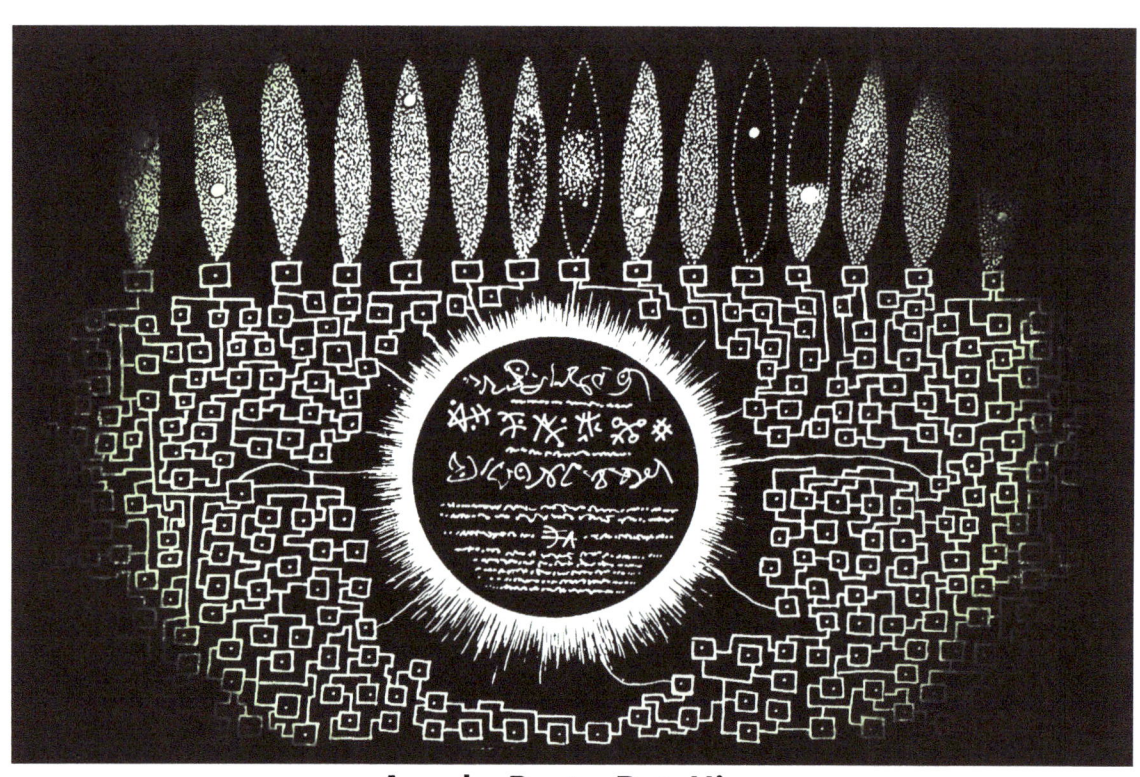

Anneke Baete: DataHive

Billy Bob Beamer: Word Dust, New River Series (328)

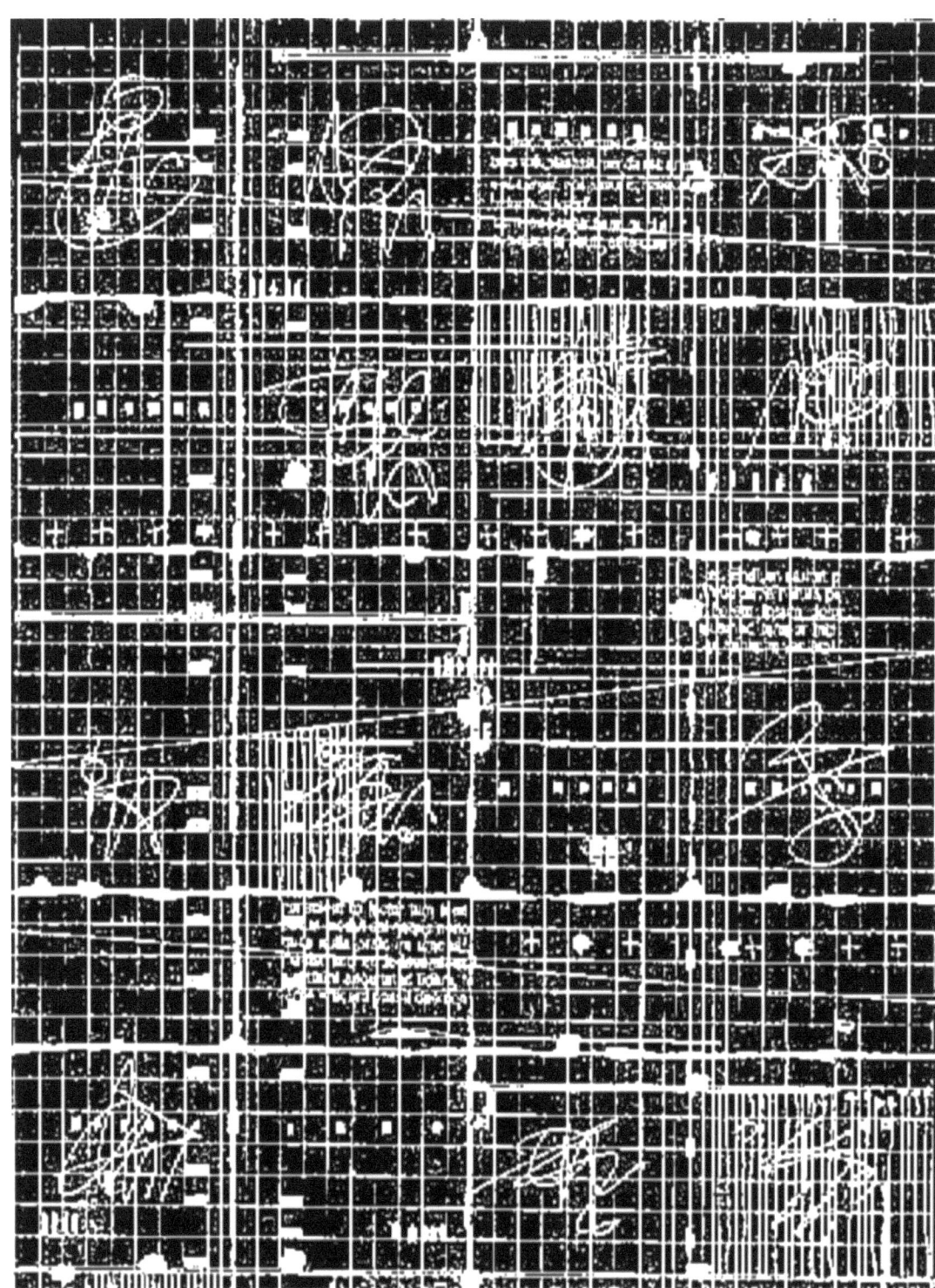

Carlyle Baker: Asemic#2

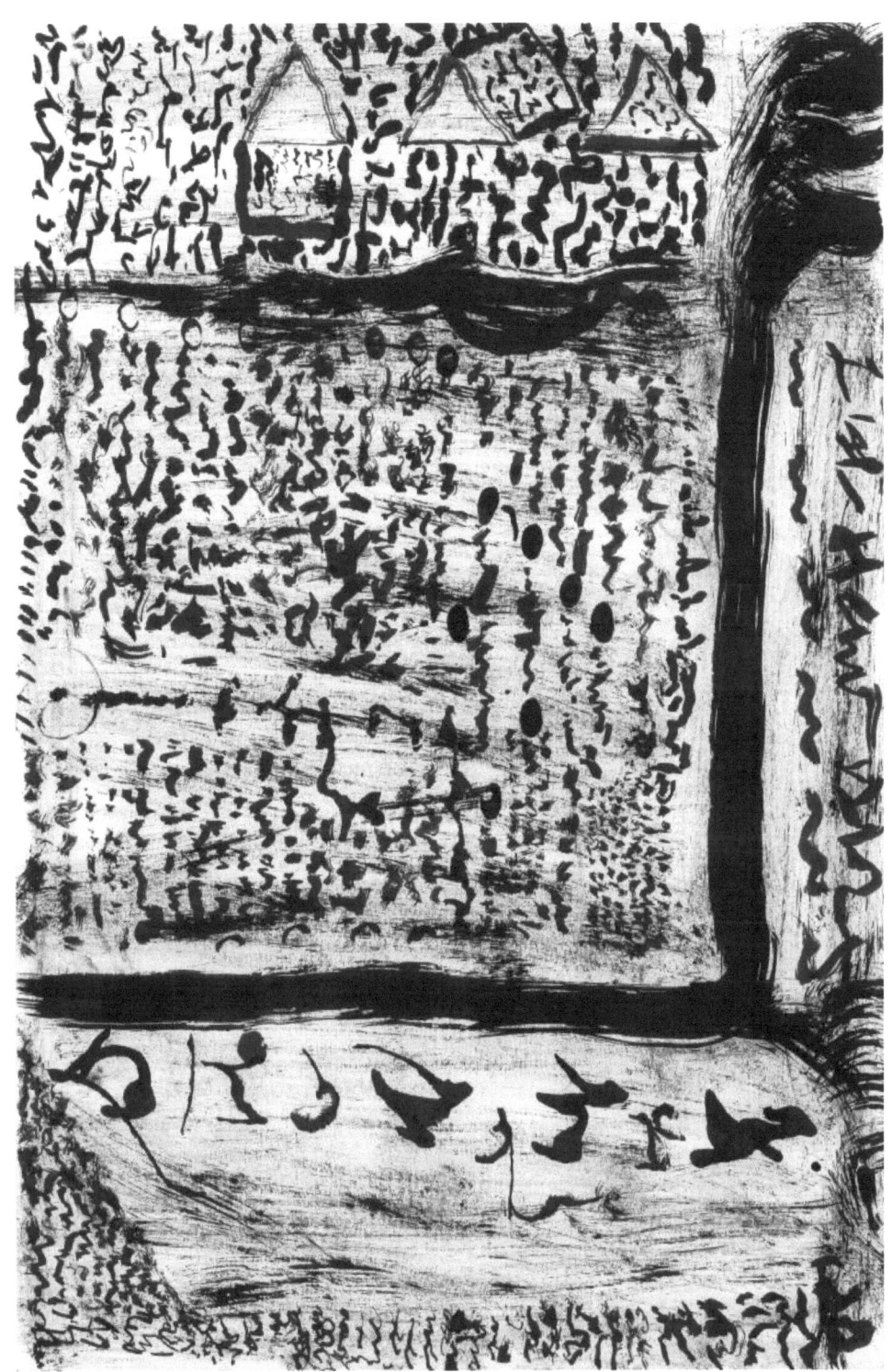

Cristiano Caggiula: Lexique De La Politique

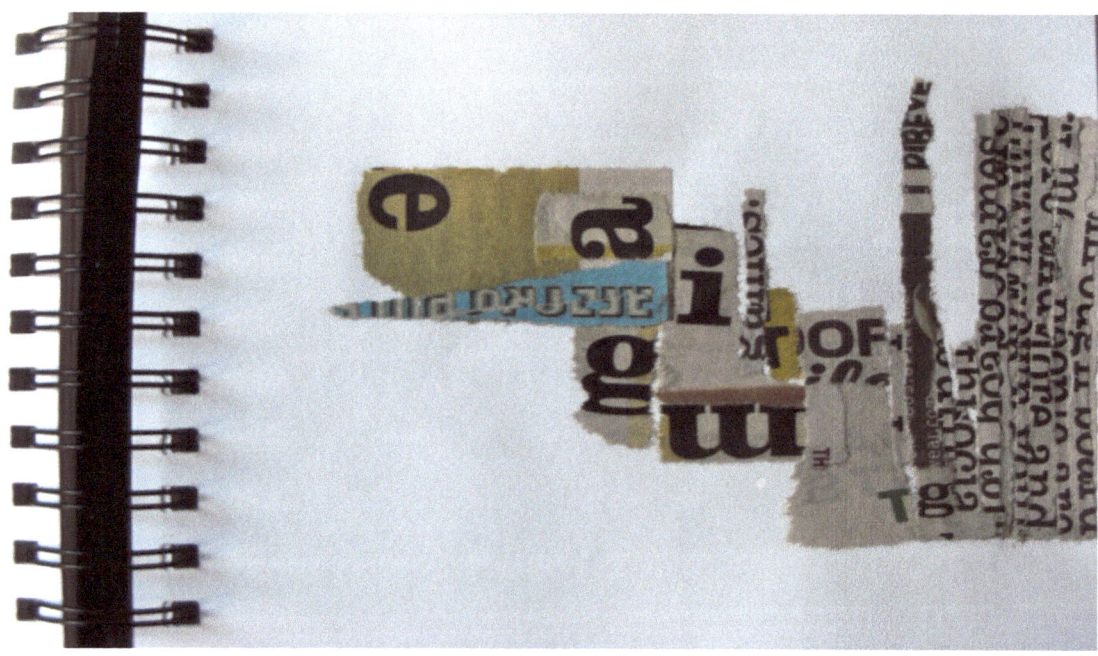

Larry Dellinger: Words

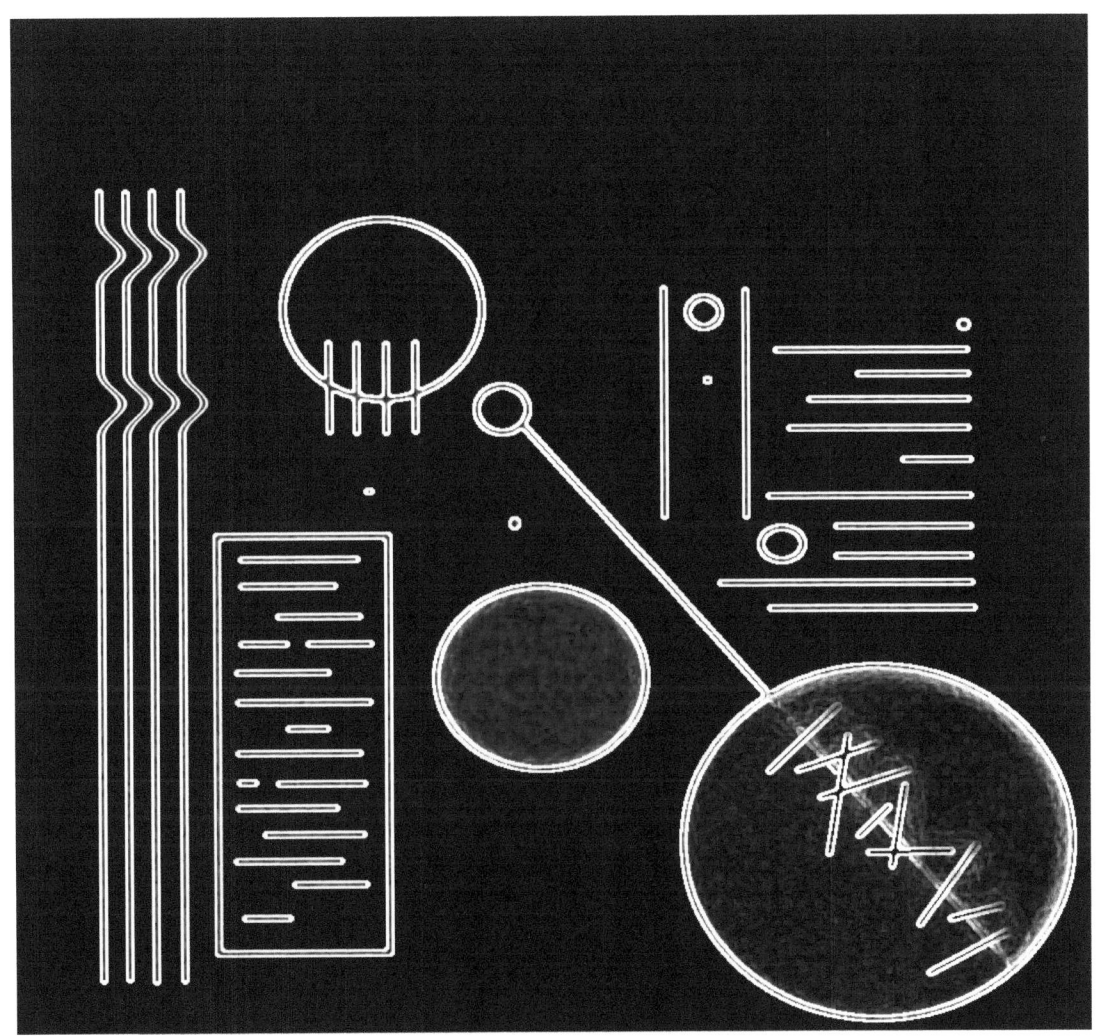

Michael Jacobson: Space News

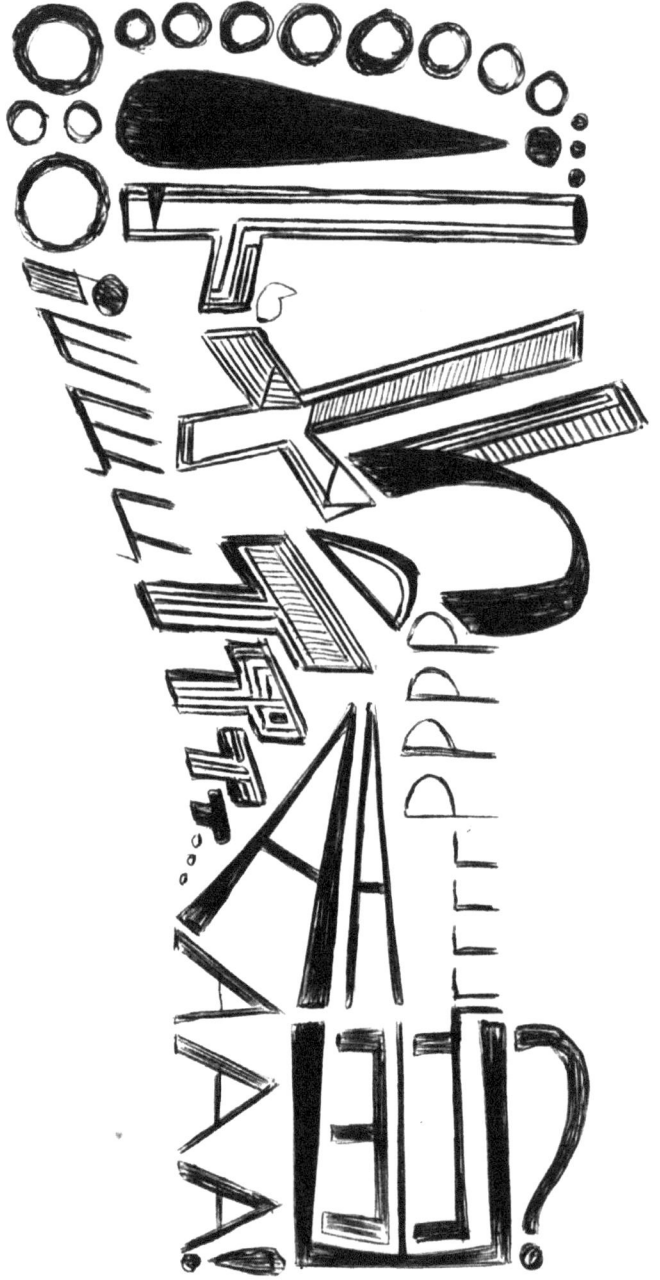

Volodymyr Bilyk: Humble Bumble Bubbles

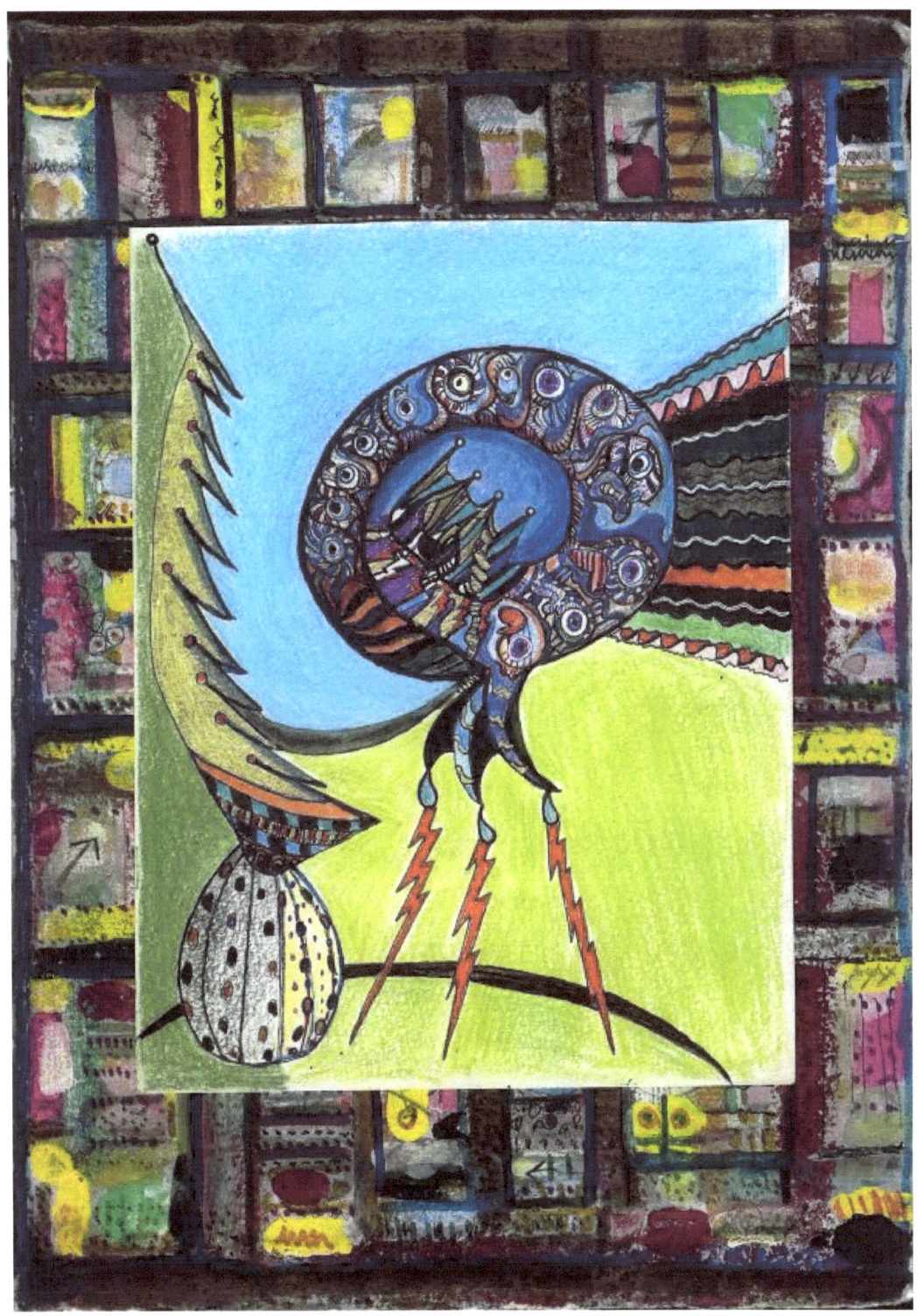

Jesse Glass: Untitled

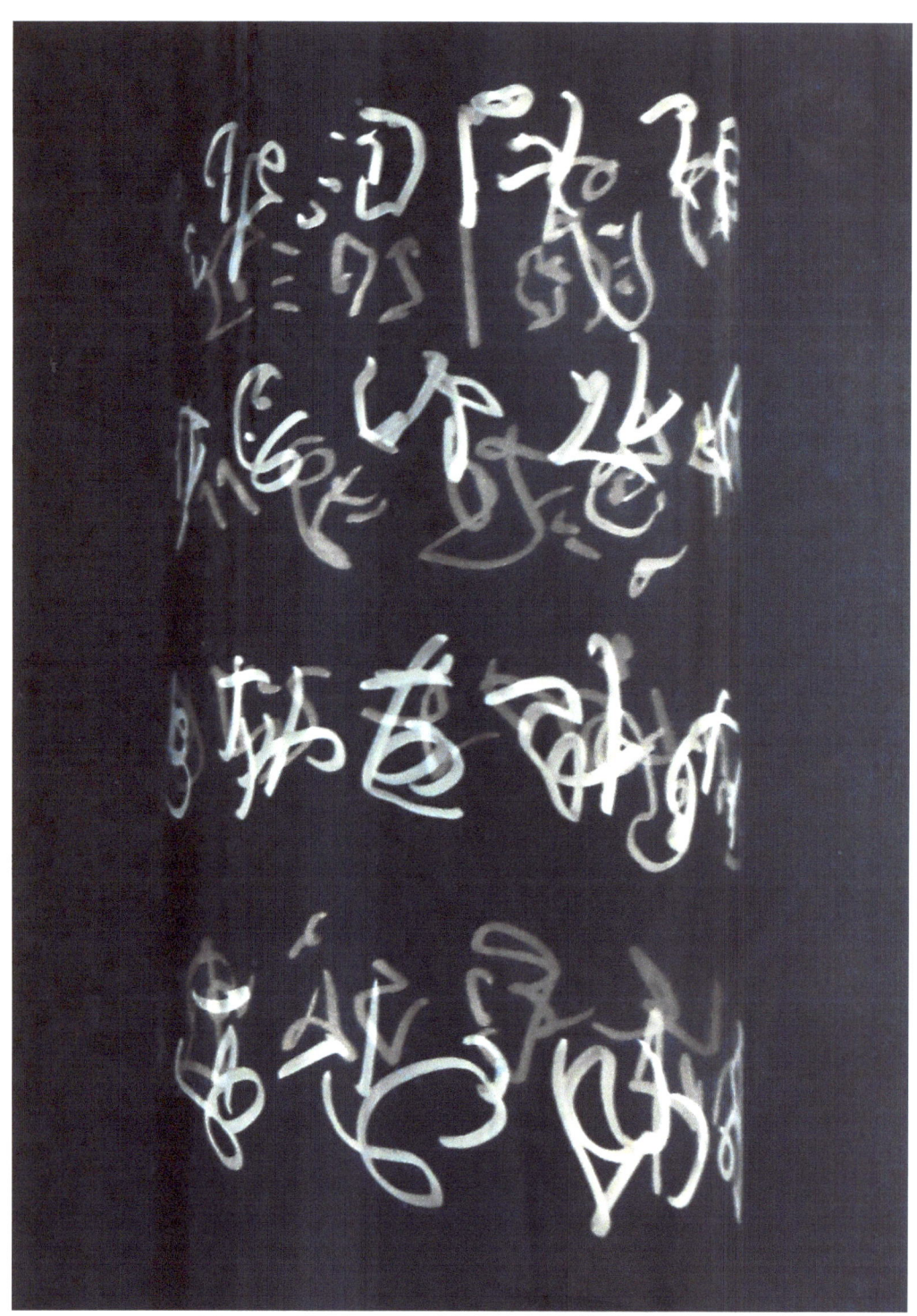

Marco Giovenale: Asemic Object 3890

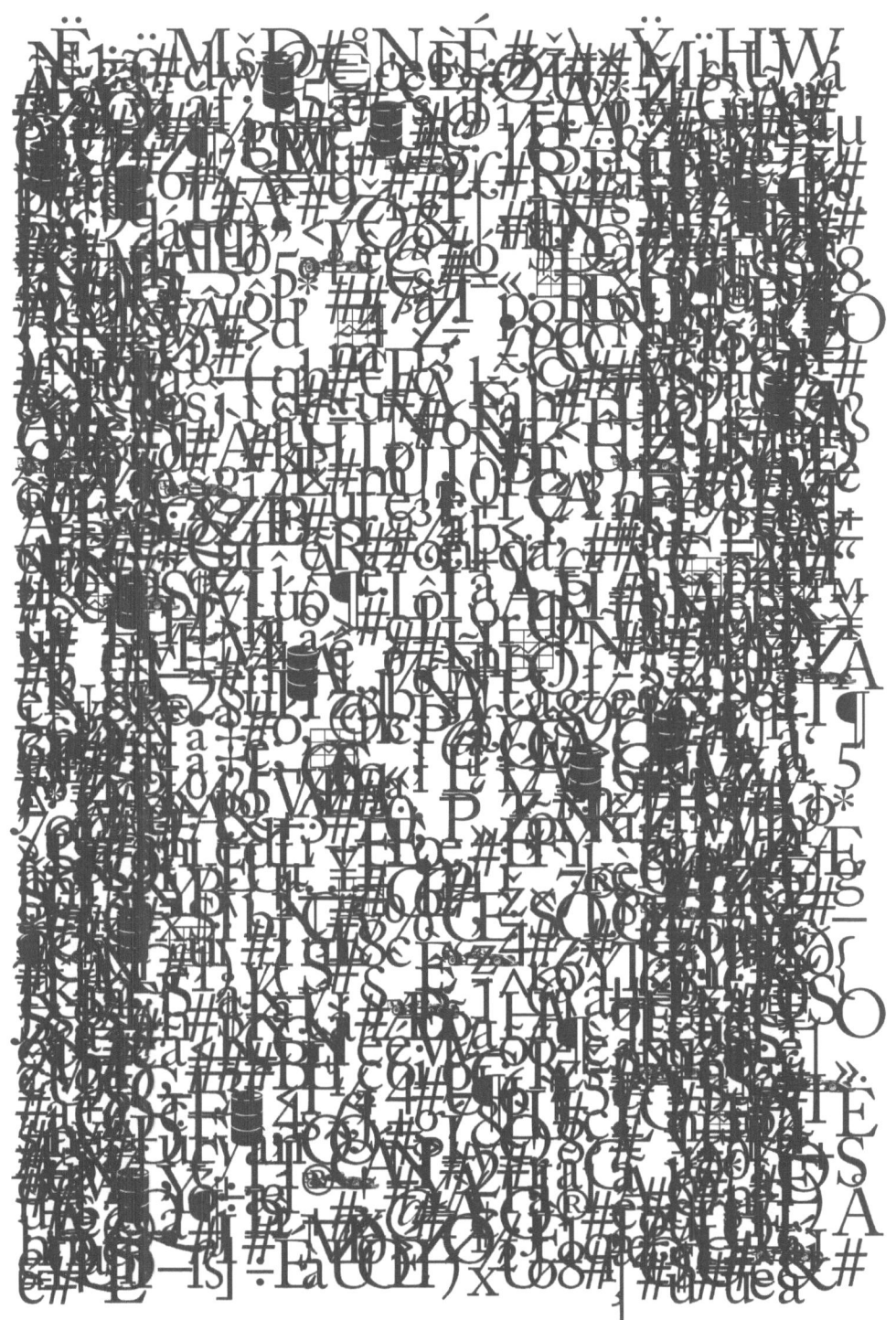

Manuel Arturo Abreu: Untitled

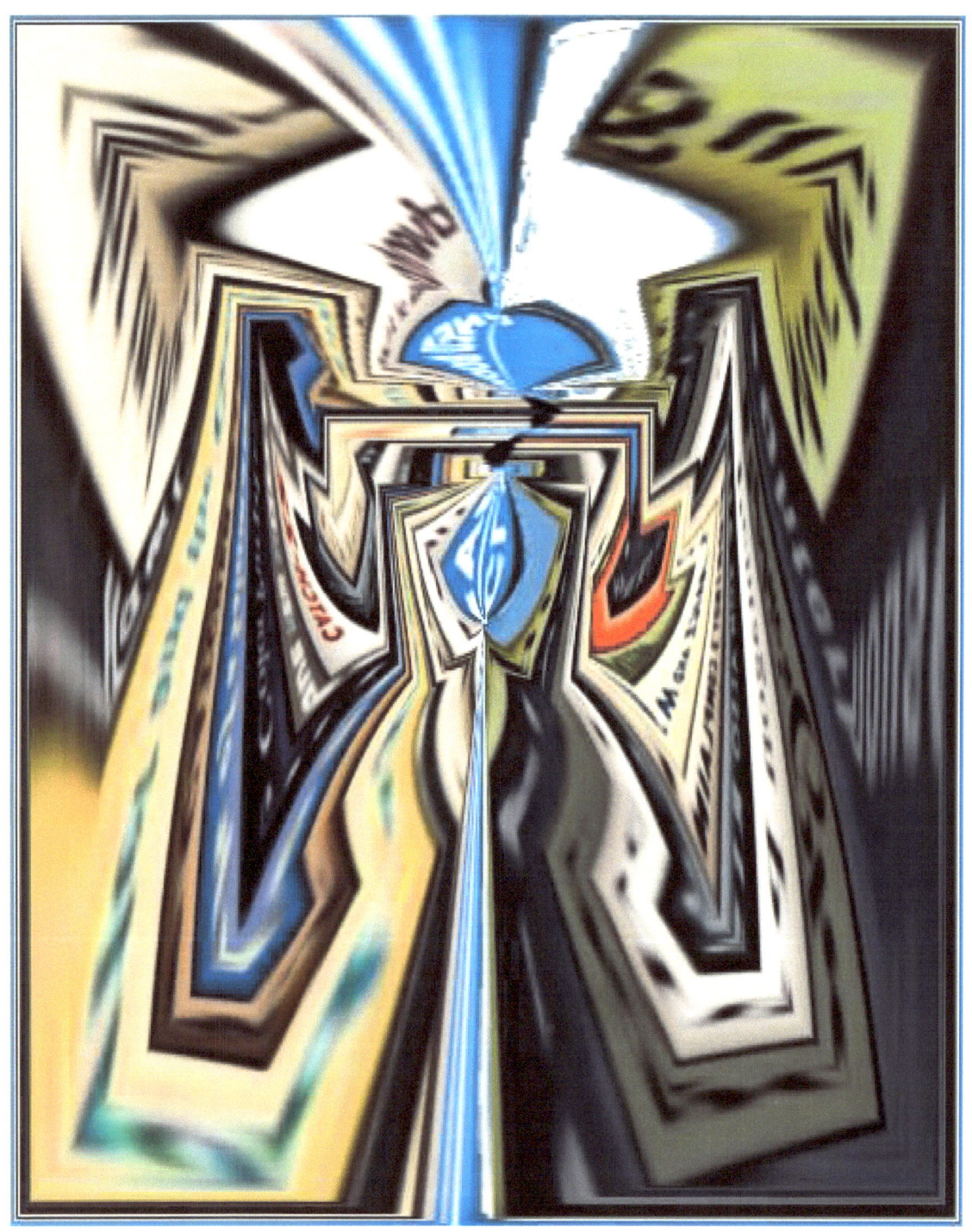

David Nadeau: An Emblem Of Peril

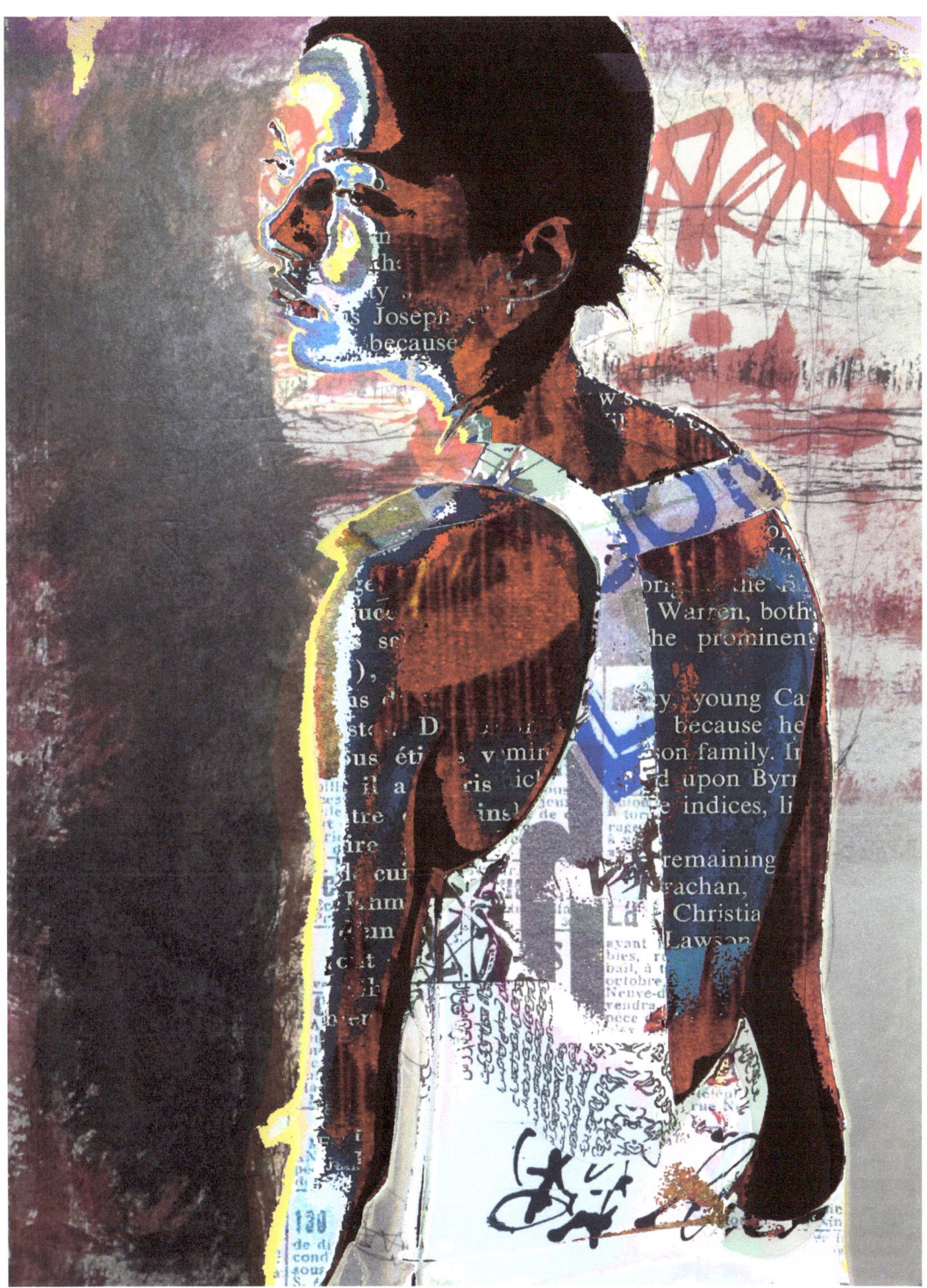

Moan Lisa: Untitled

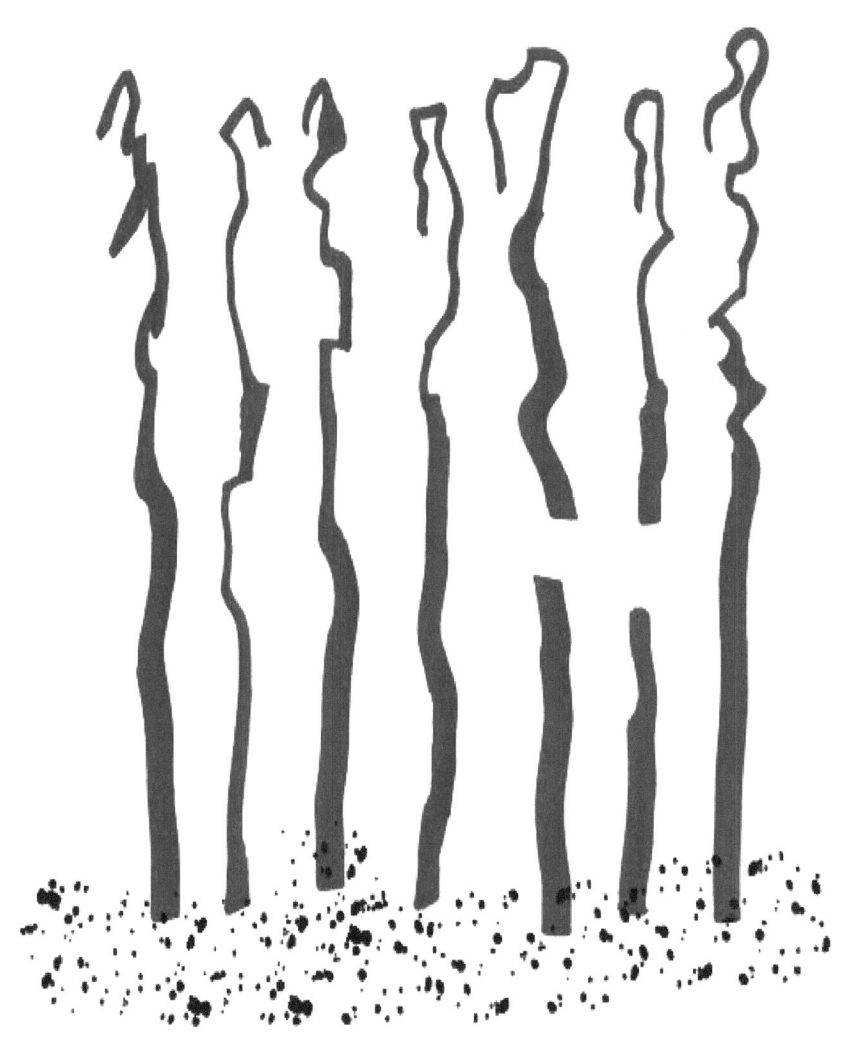

Reijo Valta: Cozy Mystery

Edward Kulemin: Fill In

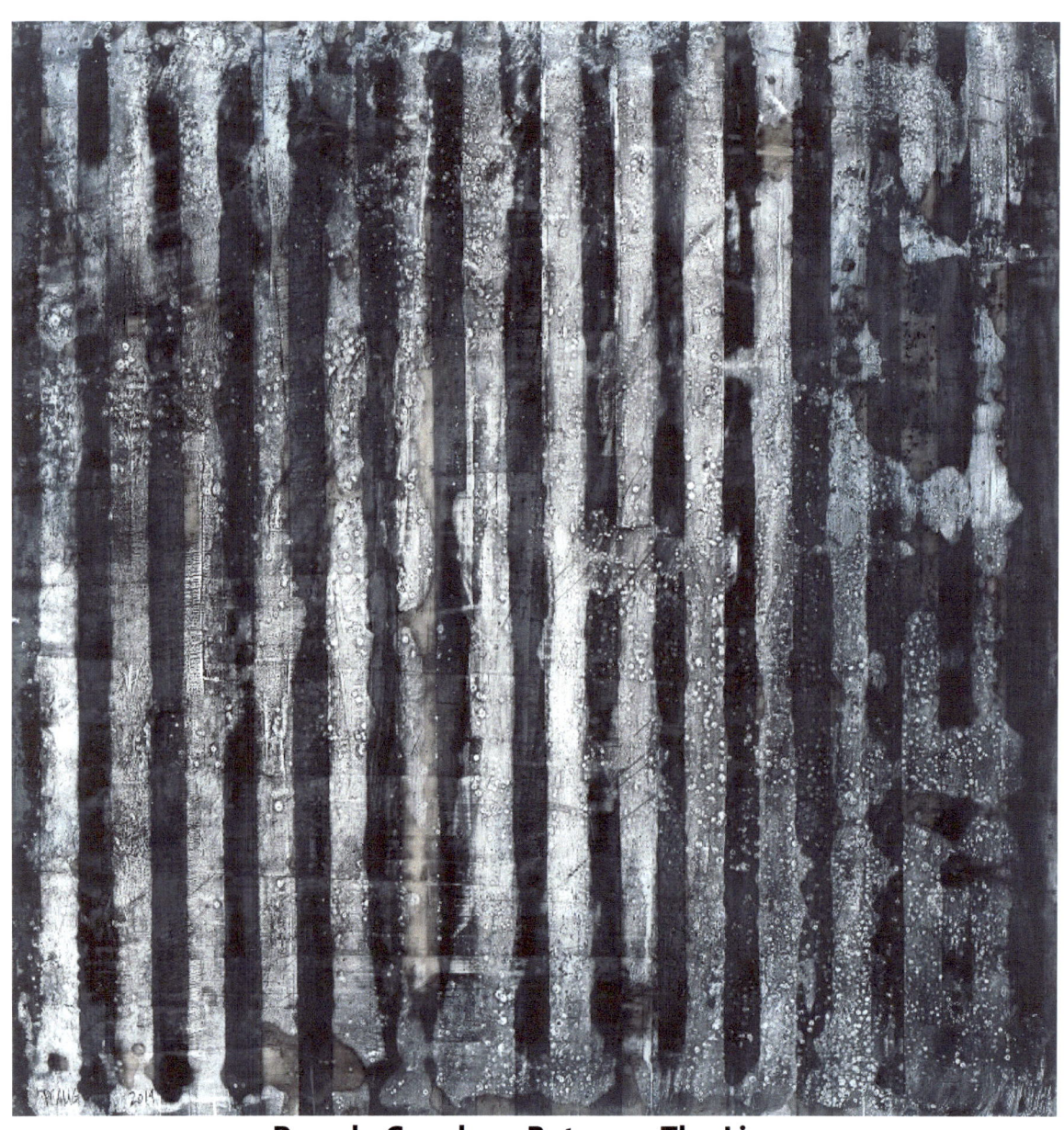

Pamela Caughey: Between The Lines

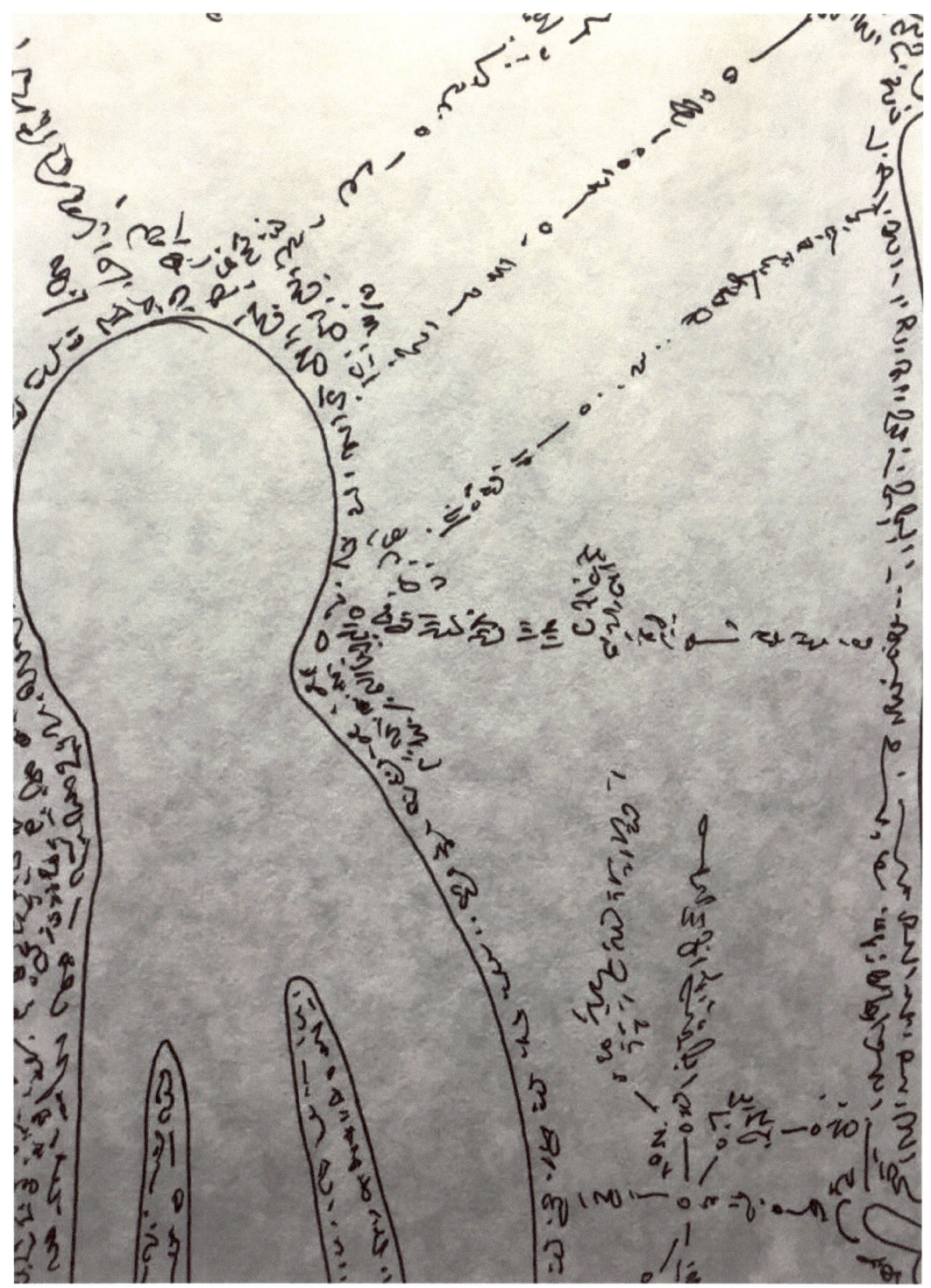

Jay Snodgrass: Telect

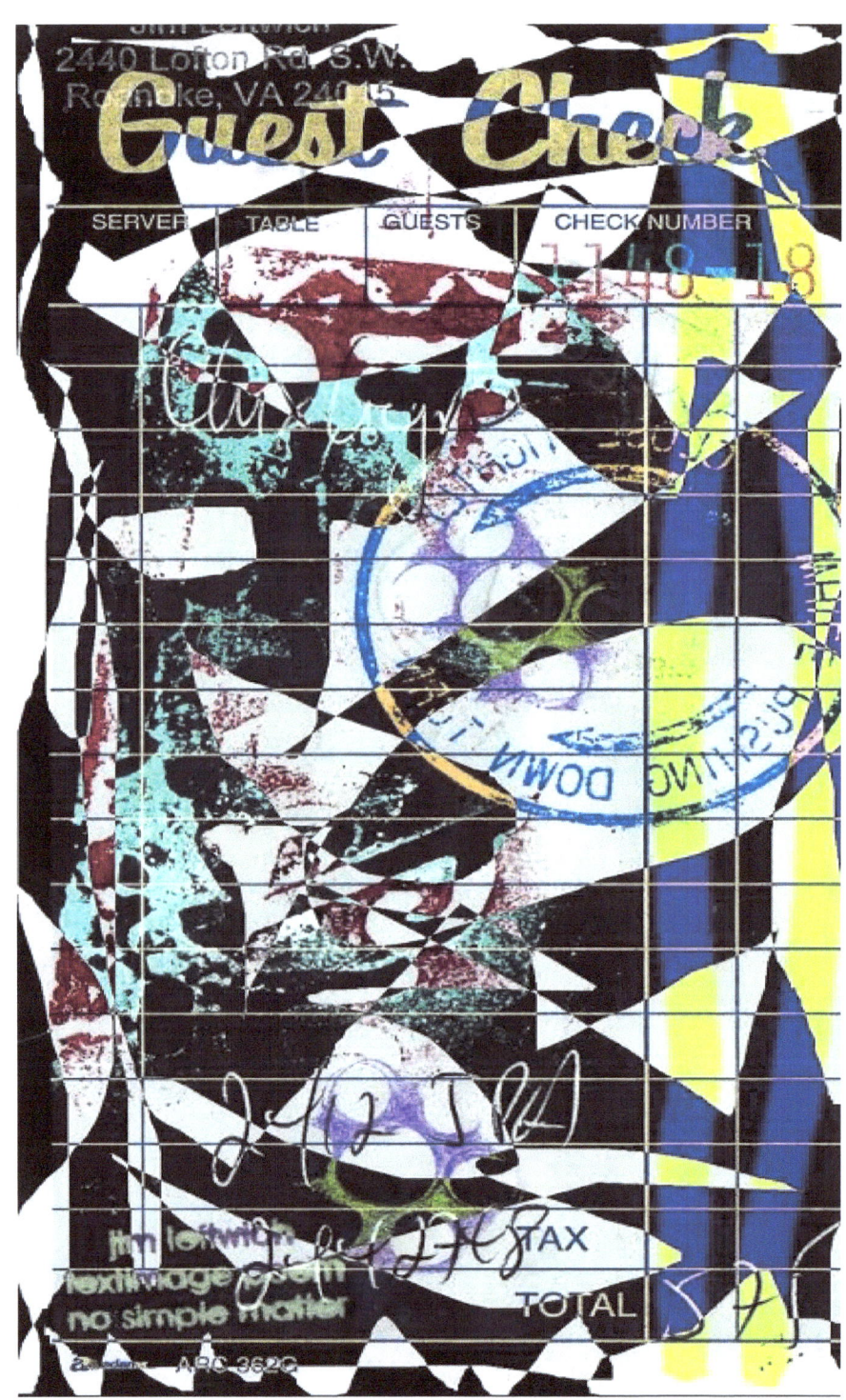

Jim Leftwich: Guest Check

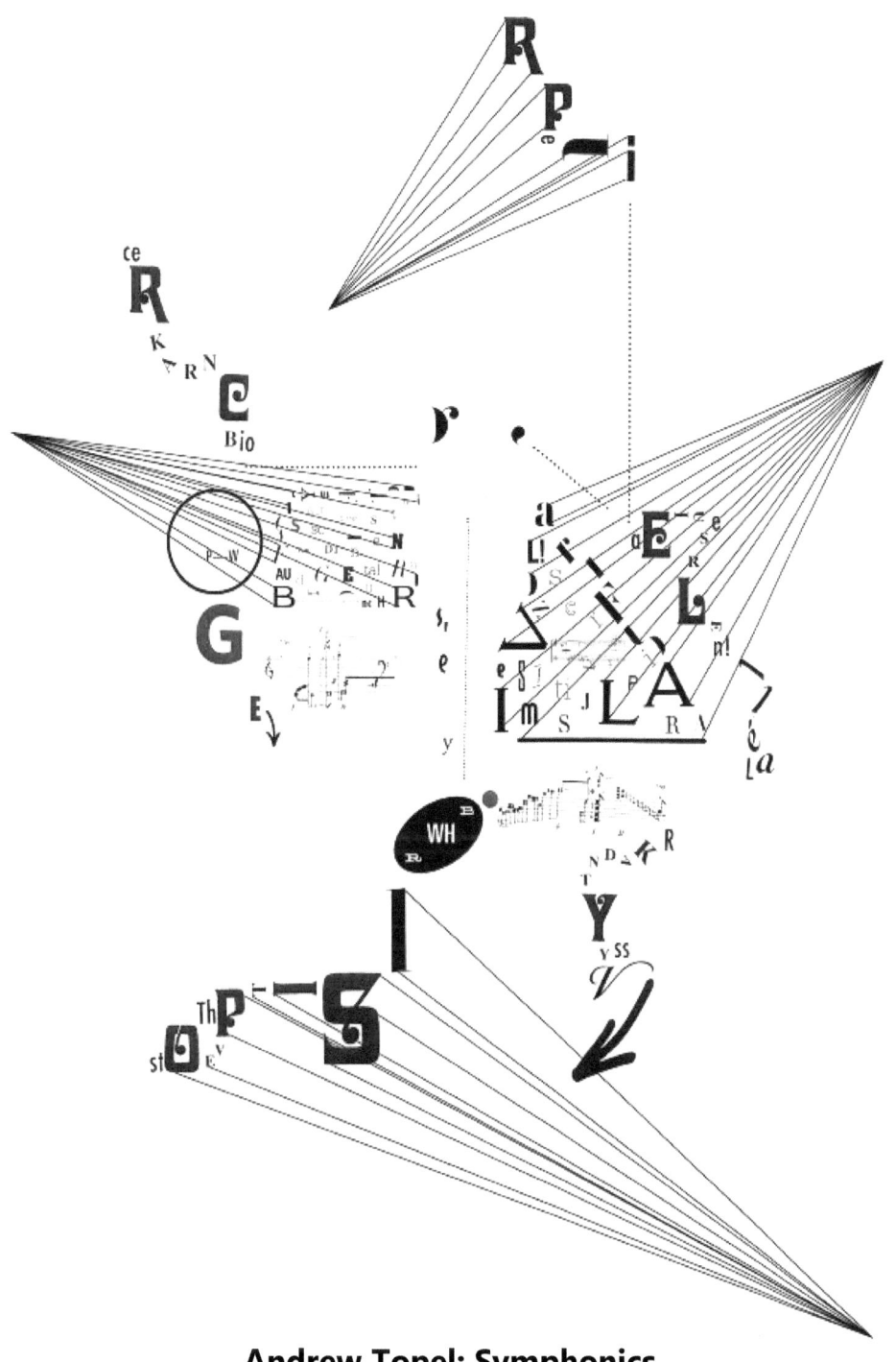

Andrew Topel: Symphonics

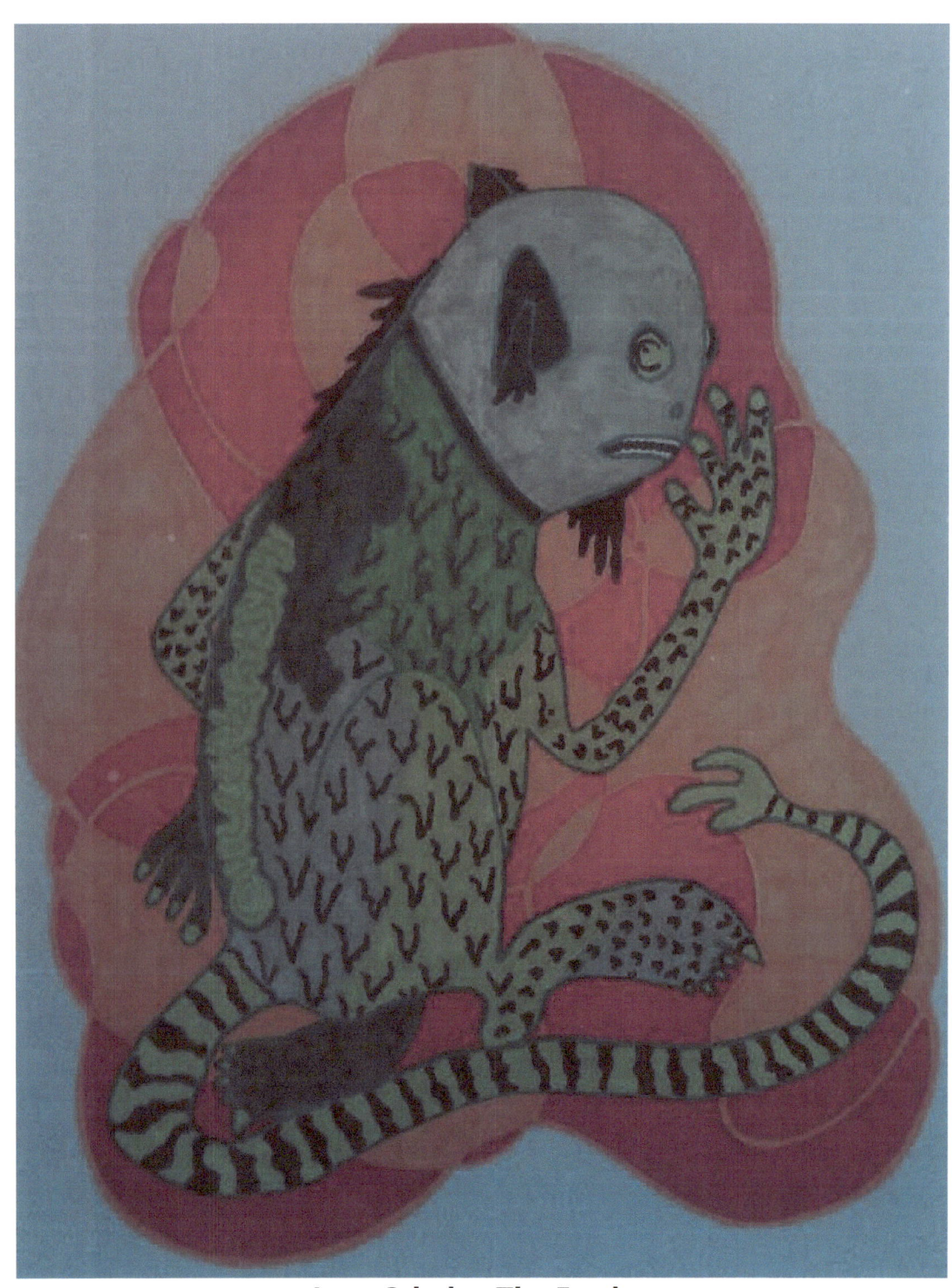

Lucy Schultz: The Feeder

ARTIST BIOGRAPHIES BY ORDER OF APPEARANCE

FRANCESCO APRILE is a poet, visual poet, journalist. In 2010 he became member of the literary movement *New Page* founded in 2009 by F. S. Dòdaro. He have founded the group of research and artistic protest *Contrabbando Poetico* (2011) and the magazine of critic and experimental languages *www.utsanga.it* (2014, with C. Caggiula). Link: http://faprile.wordpress.com. Contact: Francesco.aprile85@gmail.com.

IAN S. CROSS received a Masters of Fine Arts degree in Printmaking and Drawing in 2004 from The Ohio State University. His creative projects have varied from traditional printmaking, drawing processes and to mixed media. The underlying influences in Ian's creative efforts stem from handwriting, language structures, poetics and urban debris. His prints, drawings and mixed media artworks have been exhibited nationally, internationally and are held in museum and private collections. Contact: ic_fine_art@att.net.

CHRISTOPHER SKINNER (a/k/a LESTARET) was born in 1968 and currently lives and works in rural Norfolk, England. He is a freelance graphic designer with an MA in design practice but has also established himself as an asemic artist. To date, he has produced three original asemic novels – *four fools*, *pabulum*, and *underovary*, as well as contributing towards (and designing) the collaborative asemic graphic novel *a kick in the eye,* also included in *an anthology of asemic handwriting* as well as a number of other mixed media asemic artworks. Link: http://lestaret.com/.

CECIL B. LEE is a painter, poet and writer. Involved in the Arts since his teens, it is a life-long pursuit. Some pictures of his art can be viewed at his Facebook homepage https://www.facebook.com/m.t.mynd1 under the tab "photos." Contact: clee@elp.rr.com for any questions, comments, etc.

ED BAKER is an artist and poet who resides in Takoma Park, Md. He is 67. Contact: edbaker@sdf.lonestar.org.

TATIANA ROUMELIOTI is a self-taught artist, born in 9th November 1988. She is originally from Athens, Greece. She started creating asemic writings without any profound knowledge about them in year 2013. Her work is influenced mostly by her own vivid imagination as well as her symbolic visions and lucid dreams. Contact: tatiana9111988@gmail.com.

AMANDA EARL's visual poetry has been exhibited in Russia and Windsor. Her visual poetry chapbooks include *Bone Sapling*, a collaboration with Gary Barwin (AngelHousePress), *Of the Body* (Puddles of Sky Press), *une semaine dans la vie de l'alphabet* published in "Illiterature III" (Puddles of Sky Press), and *a field guide to fanciful bugs* (Avantacular Press). Her visual poems appear in *The Last Vispo Anthology: Visual Poetry: 1998-2008 (*mentioned on the Paris Review website, as well as the online *DrukenBoat.com's* #10 (a special issue on visual poetry); *The Volta's Evening will Come*, and *Tip of the Knife*, Bill Dimichele's site for visual art & poetry. Gary Barwin wrote about Amanda's visual poetry in the *Jacket2* article *What kind of [sic] sense is that? Amanda Earl and the Synaesthesia of Reading*. For more info about Amanda, please visit http://wwwAmandaEarl.com or connect with her on Twitter @KikiFolle.

ALI ZNAIDI (b.1977) lives in Redeyef, Tunisia. He is the author of several chapbooks, including *Experimental Ruminations* (Fowlpox Press, 2012), *Moon's Cloth Embroidered with Poems* (Origami Poems Project, 2012), *Bye, Donna Summer!* (Fowlpox Press, 2014), and *Taste of the Edge* (Kind of a Hurricane Press, 2014). You can find more about him on his blog aliznaidi.blogspot.com. Contact: aznaidi1@gmail.com.

GHEORGHE MARIAN NEGUȚU is a 27-year-old writer, visual artist and animator from Ploiești, Romania. He started creating asemic works at the age of 4 but stopped after learning the alphabet. At the age of 24, he rediscovered asemic writing and some fragments of himself. His latest work can be seen here: http://thenewpostliterate.blogspot.ro/2015/02/recent-work-from-gheorghe-marian-negutu.html. Contact: ghe.negutu@gmail.com.

GREGG SIMPSON was born in Ottawa in 1947 and grew up in the rainforest environment of the west coast. His work has been exhibited in museums and galleries in Canada, the U.S., Europe and South America and is included in over 100 private and public collections internationally. In 2012 and 2013 a retrospective of his work from 1970-1975 toured museums in Spain and Portugal. In May, 2000 he had a solo exhibition in a castle in Italy which became the subject of a BRAVO TV television documentary, *A New Arcadia, The Art of Gregg Simpson*: www.greggsimpson.com/Videos.html. Contact: greggsimpson@shaw.ca.

ANNEKE BAETEN was born in Belgium and currently resides in Sydney, Australia. She attended Monash University, Australian National University, The Royal College of Music, and The Stedelijke Kunst Akademie of Belgium, studying European literature, linguistics, music, and fine Arts. A Publishing professional for the last 23 years, she has recently left the professional arena to focus on photography and asemic work, challenging 23 years of language conventions in the process. Contact: baetenanneke@gmail.com.

NICO VASSILAKIS is an artist, poet focused on visual language compositions. He works with letters as material before and after they form into words. Vassilakis has co-edited several collections of international visual poetry and currently edits the vispo section at *Coldfront Magazine*. He has several books of poetry and maintains the website http://staringpoetics.weebly.com/. Contact: shoehorns@msn.com.

LAURA DIMITROVA was born in Sofia, Bulgaria and graduated from the National Academy of Arts, Sofia, Bulgaria in 1982. Since 1991, she has been a member of the Union of the Bulgarian Artists. In 2010, she became an Associate Professor in Decorative Arts at FPPE, St. Kliment Ohridski University, Sofia, Bulgaria. In 2013, she obtained her PhD. She works in the fields of painting, drawing, collage, paper art, and artistic textile. She lives in Sofia, Bulgaria. Contact: aura.tovasamaz@gmail.com.

billy bob beamer continues his experimental music, writing small drawings, installations, and digital asemia/visual poetry. He will be exhibiting selected recent works at the Fine Arts Center for the New River Valley in Virginia, in the summer of 2015. His current digital images can be seen in Jim Leftwich's online collection *pansemic playhouse 2015* at https://www.flickr.com/photos/textimagepoetry/collections/. Recent graphite drawings can be viewed at The Nevica Project Gallery in Chicago: thenevicaproject.com. Contact: billybobbeamer@aol.com.

CARLYLE BAKER has a tendency toward inter-disciplinary studies. You might say he has several bad habits. His medical condition is known as advanced temporal suspension. Find more of his work at *new postliterate*, *empty mirror* and *calibanonline*. Contact: bekker.karl1@gmail.com.

CRISTIANO CAGGIULA is joined in the group Contrabbando Poetico in 2011. He is the co-founder of Unconventional Press and Utsanga, a journal of language research. Contact: cristiano.caggiula@outlook.it.

LARRY DELLINGER studied composition in Los Angeles with Ernest Kanitz and in Santa Barbara with Edward Applebaum. He is a freelance composer, writing incidental music for theaters throughout the United States and Europe. These include the Old Globe Theater in San Diego, Mark Taper Forum in Los Angeles, Berkeley Repertory Theater, Oregon Shakespeare Festival, American Conservatory Theater, National Actors Theater in New York City and the Oslo Nye Theater in Norway. Many of his works have been performed on radio and television. Delinger has received eleven Los Angeles DramaLogue Critics' Awards for excellence in music composition and was a recipient of the Distinguished Service Award from Chadron State College. Contact: l.delinger@yahoo.com.

MICHAEL JACOBSON is a writer and artist from Minneapolis, Minnesota USA. His latest books are *Works & Interviews 1999-2014* and *An Anthology Of Asemic Handwriting* (Uitgeverij, 2013) which he co-edited. Since 2008 he has curated *The New Post-Literate: A Gallery Of Asemic Writing*. Recently he was interviewed by Twenty Four Hours Online. In his spare time he is trying to build a cyberspace planet for his robot called THAT. Contact: thenewpostliterate@gmail.com.

VOLODYMYR BILYK is a writer, translator. His book of visual poems was recently published in the series *This is Visual Poetry* (thisisvisualpoetry.com/?p=1151) and another book of asemic short stories *CIMESA* (whiteskybooks.blogspot.com/2013/07/volodymyr-bilyk-cimesa.html) was published in White Sky Books, and *Vispo Ay Ai Ay* published by Blank Space Press. His works have also appeared in *The New Post-Literate*, *A-Minor Magazine*, *REM magazine*, Cormac *McCarthy's Dead Typewriter*, *The Otolith*, and many others. Contact: bil_sabab@ukr.net.

JESSE GLASS lives and works in Japan. His books include *Man's Wows*, *The Passion of Phineas Gage*, *Lost Poet*, *Gaha Noas Zorge*, *Black Out In My Left Eye*, and *Peter Stubbe Selections*. More about Jesse Glass here: http://hdl.handle.net/1903.1/3010. Contact: ahadada2@jcom.home.ne.jp.

MARCO GIOVENALE lives in Rome where he works as an editor and translator. He's founder and editor of *gammm* (2006) and *asemic-net* (2011). He published some books of asemic writing and also linear prose and poems. In 2011, he took part in the Bury Text Festival (Manchester). His blog at http://slowforward.wordpress.com and an updated bibliography is available at http://slowforward.wordpress.com/2014/01/01/mgs-bibliography/. Contact: mgiovenale@gmail.com.

manuel arturo abreu (b. 1991) is a poet and artist from the Bronx, currently based in Portland. See more work at http://www.twigtech.tumblr.com. Contact: manuel.arturo.abreu@gmail.com.

DAVID NADEAU is an art historian, a poet and a visual artist living in Quebec city. He participates in the surrealist movement in the groups La Vertèbre et le Rossignol and Device Scribbles collective. He has published in *Terre Gaste* (2006), *Aghula, revista de cultura* (2006), *La Conspiration dépressionniste* (2010), *Hydrolith: Surrealist Research and Investigations* (2010, 2014), *La chasse à l'objet du désir* (2014) and *A Phala* (2015). He has published at the author *La Mémoire intraveineuse par-delà processus et saveurs* (2003), *Chantiers de l'ombre* (2007), *Décembre dans la femme* (2008) et *L'Émeraude charnelle* (2011). He is interested in alchemy, Freemasonry and indigenous traditions of North America. Link: http://lavertebreetlerossignol.wordpress.com. Contact: mercuriussulphur@gmail.com.

MOAN LISA is an artist and a poet. She lives in North Liberty, Iowa with her daughter and pet rats. She does mainly digital collage using the open source software GIMP, but also does a lot of correspondence art. Moan appeared in the first issue of FABA collage magazine, won honorable mention at a show hosted by Chait Galleries, and attended Fluxfest 2014 in Chicago. She is currently in love and using this as an opportunity to explore new avenues in artwork. Link: http://mermaid.pink. Contact: moanlisa@mermaid.pink.

REIJO VALTA is a poet and non-fiction writer. He has published experimental and visual poetry mainly in Finland. His poetry blog: http://haveatreee.blogspot.com/. Contact: reijo.valta@gmail.com.

EDWARD KULEMIN was born in 1960 (Russia). An artist, poet, author of many art-projects (texts, paintings, art objects, installations, performance, visual poetry, video art, photography, book-art, mail art...); an inspiration to and organizer of various communication creative societies (KEPNOS, Group of Unknown Artists, Smolensk School of Appologists, etc.); a participant of many art exhibitions and festivals; and and author of the books *It seems to have begun* (1994), *Odnohujstvenny Ulysses* (1995), *By the artificial way* (1998), *Multimatum* (2002), and *Lowdown* (2012). Portfolio: https://www.flickr.com/photos/113405210@N03/ Contact: klmn2002@pisem.net.

PAMELA CAUGHEY grew up in Wisconsin, where she received her BS in Biochemistry from UW-Madison in 1983. After moving with her family to Hamilton, MT in 1986, she began her serious study of art and in 2010 received her MFA in Drawing from the UMT School of Art. She works in many mediums, with a special interest in encaustic and metals. Her work has received awards, been published and shown nationally. In 2014, Missoula Art Museum featured her solo exhibition *Ubiquitous: Migration of Pathogens*. She is on the faculty of the Bitterroot College of the University of Montana in Hamilton, MT where she teaches Drawing, 2D Color and Design and Sculpture. Contact: Pamela.Caughey@mso.umt.edu.

JAY SNODGRASS teaches Composition and Rhetoric at Southwest Georgia Technical College. As a poet, he is the author of two books, *Monster Zero* and the *Underflower*. Primarily a poet, he also makes handmade books, and letterpress chapbooks and broadsides. He is interested in asemic writing and the way language can blur between being a tool for communication and a being a textured meaningful surface in its own right. He alters books, and digitally transforms his drawings in order to create poetry comics. He has an MFA from Florida International University and a PhD. in English from Florida State University. He lives in Tallahassee, FL. Link: https://jaysnodgrass.see.me/. Contact: jsnodgrass@southwestgatech.edu.

JIM LEFTWICH is a poet and mail artist who lives in Roanoke, Virginia. He is the author of *Six Months Ain't No Sentence*. Since 2008, he has been involved in organizing mail art, sound poetry, visual poetry, and noise events in Roanoke. Link: https://app.box.com/s/l76xlrg78e5s8evbi4c4. Contact: jimleftwich@gmail.com.

ANDREW TOPEL resides in florida with his beautiful wife & wonderful daughter. He edits the online journal of international visual poetry *RENEGADE*. Visit the journal at http://visualpoetryrenegade.blogspot.com/. Contact: andrewtopel@gmail.com.

LUCY SCHULTZ is a Michigan-based artist with a BFA in Painting from Michigan State University. Her cat, Suzanne, is a space cadet and recently returned from her maiden voyage to Mars. Contact: lucyhightree@gmail.com.

PAUL A. TOTH is the Founder and Publisher of Eye Am Eye Books, as well as a novelist, poet, Pop Matters columnist, communication specialist, and the author of the blog Mediaphrenia: Investigating the Mysteries of Media Literacy. His website is http://www.tothotropolis.com.
Contact: TothWorld@gmail.com.